First World War
and Army of Occupation
War Diary
France, Belgium and Germany

66 DIVISION
198 Infantry Brigade
Royal Inniskilling Fusiliers
5th Battalion
1 June 1918 - 9 May 1919

WO95/3140/1

Published by

The Naval & Military Press Ltd

Unit 10 Ridgewood Industrial Park,

Uckfield, East Sussex,

TN22 5QE England

Tel: +44 (0) 1825 749494

www.naval-military-press.com

www.nmarchive.com

This diary has been reprinted in facsimile from the original. Any imperfections are inevitably reproduced and the quality may fall short of modern type and cartographic standards.

© **Crown Copyright**
Images reproduced by permission of The National Archives, London, England, 2015.

Contents

Document type	Place/Title	Date From	Date To
Heading	WO95/3140/1		
Heading	66th Division 198th Infy Bde 5th Bn Roy Innis Fus. Jun 1918-May 1919		
Heading	War Diary 5th (Ser.) Bn Rl Inniskilling Fus Period 1st To 30th June 1918 Volume XXXVI		
War Diary	Latron	01/06/1918	01/06/1918
War Diary	Surafend	02/06/1918	04/06/1918
War Diary	Kantara	05/06/1918	17/06/1918
War Diary	Alexandria	18/06/1918	18/06/1918
War Diary	At Sea	19/06/1918	21/06/1918
War Diary	Taranto	22/06/1918	23/06/1918
War Diary	Italy	24/06/1918	26/06/1918
War Diary	France	27/06/1918	29/06/1918
War Diary	Serquex	30/06/1918	30/06/1918
Heading	War Diary 5th (Ser.) Bn. RI. Inniskilling Fus Period 1st To 31st July 1918 Volume XXXVII		
War Diary	Serquex	01/07/1918	05/07/1918
War Diary	Abancourt	06/07/1918	31/07/1918
Heading	War Diary 5th (Ser.) Bn. RI. Inniskilling Fus Period 1st To 31st August 1918 Vol No.38		
War Diary	Abancourt	01/08/1918	31/08/1918
Heading	War Diary 5th (Ser.) Bn. RI. Inniskilling Fus Period September 1st To 30th 1918 Volume NoXXXIX		
War Diary	Abancourt	01/09/1918	13/09/1918
War Diary	Bernatre	14/09/1918	20/09/1918
War Diary	Maizicourt	21/09/1918	21/09/1918
War Diary	Gd Rullecourt	22/09/1918	28/09/1918
War Diary	Corbie	29/09/1918	29/09/1918
War Diary	Harbonnieres	30/09/1918	30/09/1918
Heading	War Diary 5th (Ser.) Bn. RI. Inniskilling Fus Period 1st To 31st October 1918 Volume No XXXIX		
Map	France		
Map	Army		
Map	France		
Map	Map		
War Diary	Harbonnieres	01/10/1918	01/10/1918
War Diary	Cappy	02/10/1918	02/10/1918
War Diary	Guillemont	03/10/1918	04/10/1918
War Diary	Moislans	05/10/1918	05/10/1918
War Diary	St. Emile	06/10/1918	07/10/1918
War Diary	Le Catelet	08/10/1918	08/10/1918
War Diary	T.18.d	09/10/1918	09/10/1918
War Diary	O.36.a.7.2	10/10/1918	10/10/1918
War Diary	K.27.a.3.8	11/10/1918	12/10/1918
War Diary	Maurois	13/10/1918	13/10/1918
War Diary	Maretz	14/10/1918	16/10/1918
War Diary	K.32.b.0.9	16/10/1918	16/10/1918
War Diary	Q.2. Central	18/10/1918	20/10/1918
War Diary	Maurois	21/10/1918	21/10/1918
War Diary	Premont	22/10/1918	31/10/1918

Miscellaneous	198th Infantry Brigade		
Miscellaneous	198th Infantry Brigade Report On Operations	12/10/1918	12/10/1918
Miscellaneous	Part II	09/10/1918	09/10/1918
Miscellaneous	Part III	11/10/1918	11/10/1918
Map	Map A		
Map	Map B		
Map	Map C		
Map	Map D		
Miscellaneous	Account of Operations Part IV		
Miscellaneous	Part IV	18/10/1918	18/10/1918
Miscellaneous	Part V The Advance To The Red Line	18/10/1918	18/10/1918
Miscellaneous	Part VI The Advance To The Red Line	20/10/1918	20/10/1918
Miscellaneous	Special Order	24/10/1918	24/10/1918
Heading	War Diary 5th (Ser.) Bn. Rl. Inniskilling Fus Period 1st To 30th November 1918 Volume No XL		
War Diary	Premont	01/11/1918	02/11/1918
War Diary	Honnechy	03/11/1918	03/11/1918
War Diary	Le Cateau	04/11/1918	04/11/1918
War Diary	Pommereuil	05/11/1918	05/11/1918
War Diary	Landrecies	06/11/1918	06/11/1918
War Diary	Novelles	07/11/1918	07/11/1918
War Diary	J.3.c.9.2	08/11/1918	08/11/1918
War Diary	V.6.a	09/11/1918	10/11/1918
War Diary	Copreaux Farm	11/11/1918	12/11/1918
War Diary	Sars Poteries	13/11/1918	14/11/1918
War Diary	Clairfayts	15/11/1918	18/11/1918
War Diary	Rance	19/11/1918	19/11/1918
War Diary	Philippeville	20/11/1918	23/11/1918
War Diary	Morville	24/11/1918	24/11/1918
War Diary	Hastiere-Par-de la	25/11/1918	30/11/1918
Heading	War Diary 5th (Ser.) Bn Rl. Inniskilling Fus Period 1st To 31st December 1918 Volume No XLI		
War Diary	Hestiere Par-de la	01/12/1918	15/12/1918
War Diary	Houyet	16/12/1918	16/12/1918
War Diary	Rochefort	17/12/1918	31/12/1918
Heading	War Diary V Royal Inniskilling Fusrs Period 1st To 31st January 1919 Volume XLII		
War Diary	Rochefort	01/01/1919	31/01/1919
Heading	War Diary of 5th (ser.) Bn Rl, Inniskilling Fus From Febry 1-28/ 1919 Vol 43		
War Diary	Rochefort	01/02/1919	17/02/1919
War Diary	Rochefort	18/02/1919	28/02/1919
Heading	War Diary of 5th Royal Inniskilling Fus From March 1st To March 31st Volume No.44		
War Diary	Rochefort	01/03/1919	04/03/1919
War Diary	Sovet	05/03/1919	31/03/1919
Heading	War Diary For April 1919 5th Royal Inniskilling Fusiliers Vol XLV		
War Diary	Sovet	01/04/1919	06/04/1919
War Diary	Ciney	07/04/1919	30/04/1919
Heading	War Diary 5th Ryl Inniskilling Fusiliers May 1-9 1919		
War Diary	Ciney	01/05/1919	01/05/1919
War Diary	Antwerp	02/05/1919	09/05/1919

WO 95/3140/1

66TH DIVISION
198TH INFY BDE

5TH BN ROY. INNIS. FUS. -
JUN 1918 - MAY 1919

FROM EGYPT
10 DIVISION   31 BDE

WAR DIARY

6th (Ser.) Bn. R. Inniskilling Fus.

PERIOD.
1st to 30th June 1918

VOLUMNE XXXVI

Army Form C. 2118.

WAR DIARY
or
INTELLIGENCE SUMMARY.
(Erase heading not required.)

June (1.)

Place	Date	Hour	Summary of Events and Information	Remarks and references to Appendices
LATRON	1	1900	Battalion marched to SURAFEND Camp arriving 0030 on the 2nd. — Good march, eight miles to km.	JJE
SURAFEND	2		Coys. cleaning up — early to bed.	JJE
"	3		Coys. at disposal of Coy Commanders.	JJE
"	4	1430	Marched to LUDD station and entrained at 1745 — Very dusty tiresome journey.	JJE
KANTARA	5	0900	Battalion arrived at KANTARA Railway Station and marched to camp at 5½ Klm along DUEIDAR Road.	JJE
"	6		"A" & "B" Coys. bathing in SUEZ Canal. "C" & "D" Coys. Arms and Coy Drill.	JJE
"	7		"C" "D" Coys. bathing in SUEZ Canal. "A" "B" Coys. Coy Courses.	JJE

Army Form C. 2118.

WAR DIARY
or
INTELLIGENCE SUMMARY.
(Erase heading not required.)

Place	Date	Hour	Summary of Events and Information	Remarks and references to Appendices
KANTARA	8		Battalion marched to KANTARA and were transported by 11th La. Section - Strength 31 offs. 856 O.R. received 78 O.R. from No.2 I.B.D.	WE
"	9.		Divine Service - Battalion washing and bathing at No. 2. I.B.D.	WE
"	10.		C.Y.D. Coys bathing in SUEZ Canal - A + B at disposal of Coy. Commrs.	WE
"	11.		Coys at disposal of Coy Commrs for completion of Battalion fitted out with Small Box Respirators by So. Staff G.H.Q.	WE
"	12.			WE
"	13.	1500	Coys at disposal of O.C. Coys. Battalion washing & bathing at No. 2. I.B.D.	WE

Army Form C. 2118.

WAR DIARY
or
INTELLIGENCE SUMMARY.
(Erase heading not required.)

Place	Date	Hour	Summary of Events and Information	Remarks and references to Appendices
KANTARA	14		Coys under O°C Coys for Coy Drill etc. – Getting clothes (S.D. standing in Khaki drill).	J.J.E.
"	15		Coys under O°C Coys for inspection etc	J.J.E.
"	16	1800	Battalion marched to KANTARA West Station, entrained 2100, departed 2200.	J.J.E.
"	17	0600	Arrived at Alexandria and embarked on H.M.T. MALWA. Battalion & baggage all on board by 1100.	J.J.E.
		1700	Practice Alarm Stations.	
ALEXANDRA	18	1300	Moved from Docks & into bay – Sailed at 1330 with convoy.	J.J.E.
AT SEA	19	1000	Ship rounds – every one at Alarm posts – very good weather	J.J.E.
"	20	1000	Alarm Rounds & Alarm posts – weather good	J.J.E.

WAR DIARY
or
INTELLIGENCE SUMMARY

Army Form C. 2118.

Place	Date	Hour	Summary of Events and Information	Remarks and references to Appendices
AT SEA	21	1215	Submarine Alarm - torpedo fired by submarine but ship missed -	
		1245	All clear -	
		1315	Arrived TARANTO, Italy - moved into inner harbour about 17.30	
		1900	Commenced unloading baggage.	
TARANTO	22	0430	Battalion commenced disembarking at 0430 and marched to Rest Camp CIMINO arriving at 0600.	
		1500	Battalion bathed	
"	23	0300	Marched to CIMINO station and commenced entraining at 0900	
		0523	Train departed - Halted for 1 hour for tea at BARRI.	
ITALY	24		Train travelled along ADRIATIC Coast - Halted at FAENZA for tea etc	
"	25		Very hot day - all in train.	
"	26		Moved to Riviera Coast by Genoa etc. - Halted at VENTIMIGLIA for tea	
FRANCE	27		Passed through MARSEILLES	

Army Form C. 2118.

WAR DIARY
or
INTELLIGENCE SUMMARY.
(Erase heading not required.)

Instructions regarding War Diaries and Intelligence Summaries are contained in F. S. Regs., Part II. and the Staff Manual respectively. Title pages will be prepared in manuscript.

(5.)

Place	Date	Hour	Summary of Events and Information	Remarks and references to Appendices
FRANCE	28		Passed through outskirts of Paris - Versailles &	
"	29.		Arrived at FORGE LES EAU and encamped	
SERQUEX	30		Transport arrived from ABBEVILLE marched to SERQUEX	

3/5/18

James Paterson Lt Col
Comdg 5th R. Inniskilling Fus

WAR DIARY

5th. (Ser.) Bn. Rl. Inniskilling Fus

— PERIOD —
1st to 31st July 1918

VOLUME XXXVII

CONFIDENTIAL

WAR DIARY
or
INTELLIGENCE SUMMARY.
(Erase heading not required.)

Army –

July 1.

Place	Date	Hour	Summary of Events and Information	Remarks and references to Appendices
SERQUEUX	1.		Battalion engaged digging air-craft trench.	
"	2.		Companies out disposed of Coys. Reserve for infantry etc.	
"	3.		"A" & "B" Coys. Route marched to FORGES LES EAUX. O.T.D.	
"	4.		Coy. drill & bayonet fighting. "C" & "D" Coys. Route march to FORGES LES EAUX. O.T.D. Bayonet fighting & gas drill	
"	5.	0900	Battalion marched from SERQUEUX to ABANCOURT arriving 1330. – Very hot day.	
"	6.		Coys. digging trenches for cover from air-craft.	
ABANCOURT	7.		Battalion working at BLARGIES	
"	8.		Divine Service	

Army Form C. 2118.

WAR DIARY
or
INTELLIGENCE SUMMARY.
(Erase heading not required.)

Place	Date	Hour	Summary of Events and Information	Remarks and references to Appendices
ABANCOURT	9.		Strength 29 Officers 841 ORs. — Coys. at the disposal of Coy Commrs. for Platoon, Coy. & Physical Training parades	
"	10		Coys Training and Coy Commrs.	
"	11		"	
"	12		Inspection of A & B Coys by Commanding Officer Inspection of C & D Coys by Commanding Officer Divine Service — 1400. Battalion inspected by General Sir D. Ratinson	
"	13			
"	14.		Company Training "A" & "B" Coys. Arms and Gas drill "C" & "D" Bayonet fighting and Musketry	
"	15		"A" and "B" Coys. route march to ABANCOURT village & C "C" & "D" Coys. Musketry & Arms Drill	
"	16.			

WAR DIARY or INTELLIGENCE SUMMARY

Army Form C. 2118.

Place	Date	Hour	Summary of Events and Information	Remarks and references to Appendices
ABANCOURT	17		"A" "B" Coys. Grenade Theory & practice. "C" & "D" Coys. Co. drill & Arm drill	873.
"	18		Strength 29 Officers 839 OR. — Battalion gas mask fitted and tested by the personnel.	873.
"	19		"C" & "D" Coys. route march. "A" & "B" Coy drill.	873.
"	20		Coys. under Coy Commdrs. for inspection etc	873.
"	21		Divine Service —	873.
"	22		"A" & "B" Coys. Musketry & Bayonet fighting — "C" & "D" Coys. drill & Bombing.	873.
"	23		A & B Coys. Route march, attended by Drums. C. & D Coys. — Bayonet fighting & musketry. In afternoon, Inspection lectures by Officers. N.C.O's under R.S.M.	ff.
"	24		A & B Coys. — Bombing & musketry. C & D Coys. — Route march. In afternoon — Half-holiday. Inspection & parade R.S.M.	ff.

Army Form C. 2118.

WAR DIARY
or
INTELLIGENCE SUMMARY.
(Erase heading not required.)

Instructions regarding War Diaries and Intelligence Summaries are contained in F. S. Regs., Part II. and the Staff Manual respectively. Title pages will be prepared in manuscript.

(4)

Place	Date	Hour	Summary of Events and Information	Remarks and references to Appendices
ADANCOURT	25"		A. & B. Coys. - Gen & Semi Drill, C. & D. Coys. Bayonet Fighting & Bombing. In afternoon - N.C.Os under instruction in B.F. & P.T. First inter-Company run - each platoon represented by six runners. Run by A.Cy.	Apps.
"	26		A. & B. Coys. - Gun nastly, C. & D. Coys. Route-march, & T.D. In afternoon - Lectures by officers. N.C.Os under R.S.M.	Apps.
"	27	7-8 am 9-11	Battalion under R.S.M. Inspection of Kits. Digging-in of Tents started. Half Holiday.	Apps.
"	28.		Divine Service in trenches. In afternoon Field of Battalion manoeuvres, Inspection of Divisional Guard by G.O.C. 198th Inf. Brigade	Apps.
"	29		Battalion on duty. Ammunition & new range at DEAUVRIGEE carried-on. Baths at BEAUCOURT in afternoon, and disinfection of blankets & under-clothing.	Apps.
"	30		Baths at BEAURIES in morning. Digging-in of Tents completed. Issue of Lewis-gun, 13 rynnt-Fighting etc carried-on. Inspection of Transport by G.O.C. 198th Inf. Brigade	Apps.

WAR DIARY
or
INTELLIGENCE SUMMARY.

Army Form C. 2118.

Place	Date	Hour	Summary of Events and Information	Remarks and references to Appendices
ASHHURST	31 July		Firing on 30° range till 3 p.m. Two practices Gregory & application. Inter-Platoon run — 19th Inf Bayonets won by Battalion.	

J.S. Paterson
Lieut Col
Comdg 5th (Ser.) Bn. Rl. Inniskilling Fus

20.I.

9/23

War Diary

5 (Ser.) Bn. Rl. Inniskilling Fus.

Period 1st to 31st August 1918

Vol. No. 38.

WAR DIARY or INTELLIGENCE SUMMARY

Army Form C. 2118.

(Erase heading not required.)

Place	Date	Hour	Summary of Events and Information	Remarks and references to Appendices
AGINCOURT	August 1st		Coys. at Company training under 2 Instructors from Training Centre. Troops on "ALERT" zone.	Appx.
"	2nd		Battalion route march in morning — Coy. training in afternoon. Prgm. 9 a.m. Held M.C. arranged Tournament. Bn. 2nd 11 Palm. Dso. 1st O.R. on leave.	Appx.
"	3rd		In morning A & B Coys. musketry 9-11 am. Both at BEAURAINS in afternoon.	Appx.
"	4th		Further musketry of "A" "B" Coys. Brigade parade service on football ground 6 at 10 am. Afternoon battalion marched past B.G.C.	Appx.
"	5th		Battalion route march. In afternoon talked volume for A.O. officers. Hockey & polo though army Rifles useful.	Appx.
"	6th		Battalion inspected by commanding Officer. Divn A.S. evening invalided Rifle run.	Appx.
"	7th		Battalion inspected by G.O.C. 66th Divn. officers marching past on return from BEAURAINS in afternoon.	Appx.

Army Form C. 2118.

WAR DIARY
or
INTELLIGENCE SUMMARY.
(Erase heading not required.)

Instructions regarding War Diaries and Intelligence Summaries are contained in F. S. Regs., Part II. and the Staff Manual respectively. Title pages will be prepared in manuscript.

Place	Date	Hour	Summary of Events and Information	Remarks and references to Appendices
ABANCOURT.	8		"A" "B" "D" Coys. bathing in evening - General working party in Camp duty. - "C" Coy. orderly	WE
"	9.		Coys. on Range, Drill & Bayonet fighting.	WE
"	10.		Battalion Route March in morning - Officers tactical scheme	WE
"	11.		afternoon	WE
"	12		Strength - 30 Officers 853 O.Rs. - Divine service	WE
"	13.		Brigade Training programme continued	WE
"			Lecture by Div. Commander - Coys on range firing graphic	WE
"			and application	WE
"	14		Collective training on High ground W. of Camp - Bright firing	WE
"			on Range	WE

"WAR DIARY or INTELLIGENCE SUMMARY." Army Form C. 2118.

Place	Date	Hour	Summary of Events and Information	Remarks and references to Appendices
ABANCOURT	15.		Battalion on Long Range all day – Great improvement in shooting.	Appx.
"	16.		Bath's arriving – Bombing & P.F.T.S. in ofternoon – Lecture on Ridge – Officer Tactical scheme "Night Outposts". Lecture on Artillery by G.O.C. Brigade. GN1703	Appx.
"	17.		Route march to LANNOY – FRETTENCOURT – LA GACHELE down return to camp.	Appx.
"	18.		Divine service – Strength. 32 Officers 864 O.Rs.	Appx.
"	19.		5 Officers 261 O.Rs proceeded to UK for fortnight's leave. Bath at BLARGIES in ofternoon	Appx.
"	20.		2 Officers 104 O.Rs proceeded to UK for fortnight leave. Bath at BLARGIES in ofternoon.	Appx.
"	21.		Battalion route march to LANNOY – ST VALLERY – VILLERS HAUDRICOURT – CUILLIERE – Camp – exceptionally hot day	Appx.

WAR DIARY
or
INTELLIGENCE SUMMARY.
(Erase heading not required.)

Army Form C. 2118.

Place	Date	Hour	Summary of Events and Information	Remarks and references to Appendices
ABANCOURT	22		Gas drill under Gas Officer until 10.00 - Retarded enter drill remainder of morning - Staff ride in afternoon for Platoon Commanders. Musketry on Long Range all day - Shooting greatly improved	J.E.
"	23			J.E.
"	24		Bayonet fighting and Bombing.	J.E.
"	25		Divine Service - Strength 32 Officers 846 O.Rs.	J.E.
"	26		Battalion bathing at BLARGIES	J.E.
"	27		Individual training on High ground W. of Camp.	J.E.
"	28		1 Officer 264 O.Rs proceeded on leave to UK.	J.E.
"	29		1 Officer 646 O.Rs on leave - UK remainder of Battalion employed on camp improvement.	J.E.
"	30		Eight Officer reinforcements joined from Base Depot, Calais.	J.E.
"	31		Strength 41 Officers 852 O.Rs.	J.E.

Jno. S. Vancouver Lt Col
Comdg. 5. R. Innis. Fus.

1-9-18

No 79

21.I.

WAR DIARY

5th. (Ser.) Bn. Rl. Inniskilling Fus.

—— PERIOD ——

September 1st to 30th
1918

VOLUMNE NO. XXXIX

CONFIDENTIAL

WAR DIARY
or
INTELLIGENCE SUMMARY.

(Erase heading not required.)

Army Form C. 2118.

September (1.)

Place	Date	Hour	Summary of Events and Information	Remarks and references to Appendices
ABANCOURT	1.		Divine Service — 41 Officers 853 O.R. (Battalion Strength)	1925.
"	2.		All available men working on Camp improvements	1925.
"	3.		Bathing at BLARGIES	0925.
"	4.		3 Officers 101. O.R. returned from Leave. U.K.	1925.
"	5.		Coys. paraded into Company Commanders for inspection	0925.
"	6.		General clean up. Battalion tactical scheme in afternoon	0925.
"	7.		Gas drill — 1 Officer 93 O.R. returned	
"			Musketry. Bayonet fighting from leave U.K.	
"	8.		Divine Service — Strength 46 Officers 906 O.R.	1925.
"	9.		Two Coys. firing on Range — Two Coys. on bombing ground	1925.

WAR DIARY
or
INTELLIGENCE SUMMARY.

Army Form C. 2118.

Place	Date	Hour	Summary of Events and Information	Remarks and references to Appendices
ABANCOURT	10		Rained heavily all day. Inspection by Coy. Commrs. carried out in tents	ByE
"	11.		Battalion bathing at BLARGIES	ByE
"	12		Battalion paraded at 11.45pm and marched to FORMERIE Stn & entrained to AUXI-LE-CHATEAU - Rained all the way to station.	ByE
"	13 April		Entraining completed. Train arrived AUXI-LE-CHATEAU at 1130 - Detrained and breakfasted on station.	
	14.00		Marched to billets - B₂ & B₁ Coys. killed in BERNATRE - "C" Coy. PROUVILLE - "D" Coy. MAIZICOURT - "A" & "B" Coys. (nettoyages) at billets	ByE
BERNATRE	14.		Coys. cleaning up & (nettoyages) at billets	ByE
"	15		Coy. Commrs. inspections, etc	ByE

WAR DIARY
or
INTELLIGENCE SUMMARY.
(Erase heading not required.)

Army Form C. 2118.

Place	Date	Hour	Summary of Events and Information	Remarks and references to Appendices
BERNATRE	16.		Position to be occupied by Battalion during Canal Corps Manoeuvres when to own jets	J.E.
"	17.		Battalion: position to operation by 0830. Front occupied by Battalion N. of ROUGEFAY to S. of BERNAVILLE	J.E.
"	18.		CANDAS - Operations ceased 4pm - "D" Coy moved to MAIZICOURT and Battalion thus billeted at HEINCOURT and MAIZICOURT. "B" + "C" Coys moved from ROUGEFAY and PROUVILLE respectively.	J.E.
"	19.		Coys. cleaning up etc. "A" "D" Coys platoon training	J.E.
"	20.		Battalion concentrated at 0800 at MAIZICOURT and marched to BARLY - arrived 1200 - Battalion rested its billets by 1230. Rained every march	J.E.
MAIZICOURT	21		Battalion marched to GRAND RULLECOURT - left BARLY 0900 arrived GD RULLECOURT 1345 - very long + wet march	J.E.

WAR DIARY
or
INTELLIGENCE SUMMARY.
(Erase heading not required.)

Army Form C. 2118.

Place	Date	Hour	Summary of Events and Information	Remarks and references to Appendices
Ed. RULLECOURT	22		Divine Service — Strength — Officers 46 O.Rs. 879.	879.
"	23		Intensive Training (Platoons) commenced in morning - afternoon digging rifle bombing.	nil
"	24		Company Training in morning - afternoon intensive digging and rifle bombing.	nil
"	25		Company Training — Baths &c.	nil
"	26		Battalion Route March with Transport - Battalion left Katry to be at 9.10 am arrived back & billet 12.45 L. Brealey Brigade Route March	nil
"	27			nil
"	28	0900	Battalion marched from Ed. RULLECOURT to PETIT HOUVIN and entrained for CORBIE and. - Very bad march - entrained about 9 p.m.	nil
CORBIE	29.	0600	Arrived CORBIE and marched to FOUILLOY — 12.45 Battalion marched from FOUILLOY to HARBONNIERES	nil
HARBONNIERES	30		Coys ind Coy. Commdrs for Platoon Training - 1945 Lecture by O.C. Brigade	J.W.B. Paterson Lieut Col Comdg 5th (Can.) Bn. C. Forestry Corps F35

WAR DIARY

5th. (Ser.) Bn. Rl. Inniskilling Fus

PERIOD.

1st to 31st October 1918.

VOLUMNE No. XXXIX

CONFIDENTIAL.

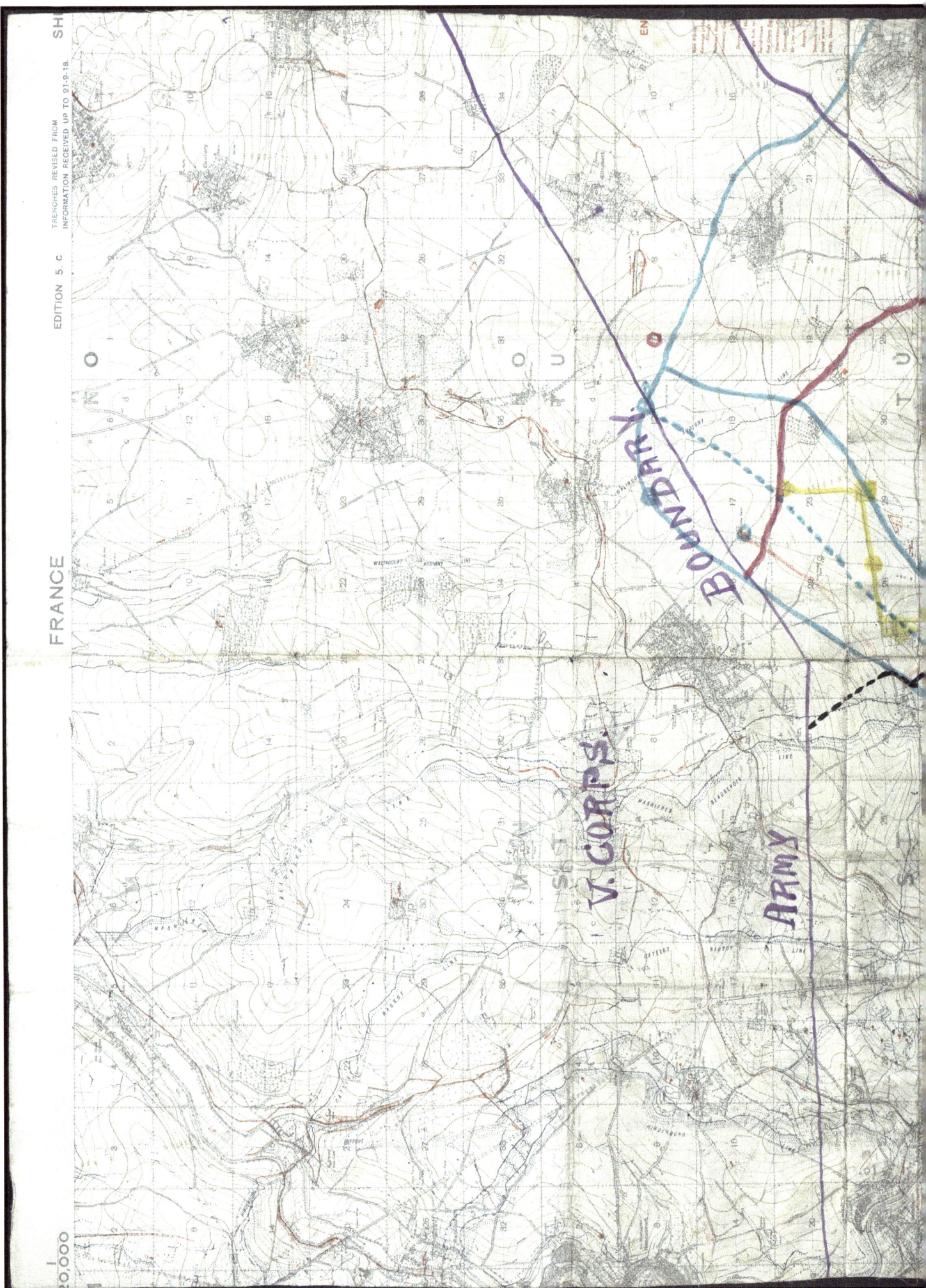

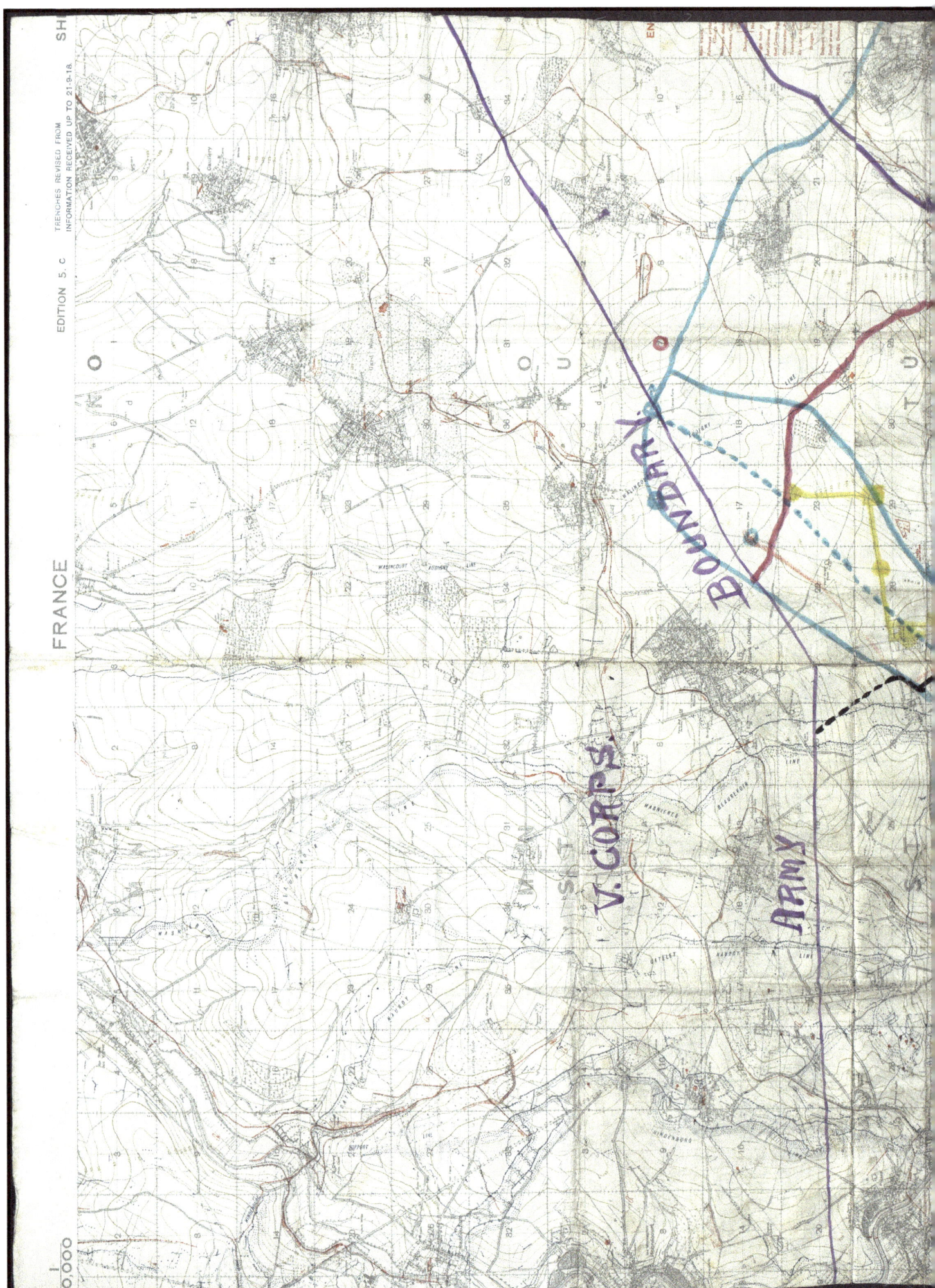

Army Form C. 2118.

WAR DIARY
or
INTELLIGENCE SUMMARY.
(Erase heading not required.)

October (1.)

Instructions regarding War Diaries and Intelligence Summaries are contained in F. S. Regs., Part II. and the Staff Manual respectively. Title pages will be prepared in manuscript.

Place	Date	Hour	Summary of Events and Information	Remarks and references to Appendices
HARBONNIERES	1		Battalion marched from HARBONNIERES to CAPPY on SOMME Canal.	W.J.
CAPPY	2		Battalion marched from CAPPY to GUILLEMONT, and billeted near TRONES WOOD — Practiced an attack en route	W.J.
GUILLEMONT	3		Training — Battalion dug trench to trench attack — afternoon, Platoon attacking "strong points" under cover of Smoke Barrage (rifle grenades) very successful	W.J.
"	4	1845	Battalion marched to MOISLAINS having started from at	W.J.
MOISLAINS	5	0945	Marched to ST. EMILE 'B' Coys. left behind	W.J.
ST EMILE	6		Inspection etc. by Coy. Comm.	W.J.
	7	1005	Battalion marched to LE CATELET and concentrated in trenches A.17.a.6.9 to Railway A.11.c.6.4 (HINDENBURG RESERVE LINE)	W.J.
		2300	Marched to take the	

WAR DIARY or INTELLIGENCE SUMMARY

Army Form C. 2118.

Place	Date	Hour	Summary of Events and Information	Remarks and references to Appendices
LE CATELET	8		Order of march en route to Take line "D"."A"."B"."C"."H.Q." - going difficult, progress slow. On 0130 when the head of "D" Coy Coln about B2 of T.P. Coming front down a counter barrage along his first leading Coy. This caught in the barrage and the advance was halted at Keep down, the barrage existed in intensity but did not stop us till 0330. Battalion formed up on the tapes at 0440. Zero 0510. Barrage opened & attacking Coys closing up to it as arranged. 0600 advance reached LA SABLONIERE and continued to HAMAGE FM. where a slight check occurred owing to enemy M.G. fire, there were influences by tanks. Led by the arrival of tanks at 0705 completed the clearing up at about 0730 of the trench T.24.A.18. and on /a/ or T.18.6.4 were in possession of the Battalion. 1245. Orders received to continue attack on GREEN LINE - Pgn. H.Qrs. reserve Coy. arrived formed to enemy trench T.18.A. 1300 attack well away 1604 O.C.'B'. Coy. reported "strong point N. of LAMPE Fm. established and 'A'.B.'D'. Coys deploying - Capt J.	Appx. Attached J.E.

WAR DIARY or INTELLIGENCE SUMMARY

Army Form C. 2118.

(3)

Place	Date	Hour	Summary of Events and Information	Remarks and references to Appendices
T.18.d.	9	0510	Orders from Bde. Ops. to SERAIN with "C" Coy + "B" HQrs only "A" "D" + "B" Coys brought on from LAMPE Fm. by Xt. Johnston on to 6th Lancs Fm. in 0.14.c.6.5 at 0545 and embussed at ELINCOURT – 0530 ABD Coys joined Battn. near ELINCOURT Cemetery. 0920 moved on in support to 6th Lancs. Fm. reached K.31.c. Ordered to Bde. reserve and rested at 0.36.a.7.2.	MJE
0.36.a.7.2.	10	0300	Moved to Startg. Point (EPINETTE) followed 6th Lancs Fm. along road to REUMONT. 0615 formed up in support to 6th Lancs. Fm. on N. of village – right flank on road. – 0645 Began to advance – enemy shelling + enfilade from right flank. numerous casualties. 0810 Reached BEAUMONT – Le CATEAU Rd. and came under very heavy artillery fire from high ground N. of Le CATEAU	
		0900	Battn. disposed as follows :– "A" "B" Coys centre + back : K.27.d.3.3 to 3.6. "C" + "D" Coys on left : K.26 d.3.8 to K.26.d.9.1. HQrs. K.26.d.3.P.	
		1000	HQrs moved onto "C" Coy.	MJE

WAR DIARY or INTELLIGENCE SUMMARY.

Army Form C. 2118.

Place	Date	Hour	Summary of Events and Information	Remarks and references to Appendices
K27a.3.8.	11th	1800	"A" "B" "C" Coys. moved off into orders of O.C. 6th Lanc. Fus. to take MONTAY. 2400 Coys & Lewis Guns. back in old position under Bank.	J.E.
"	12		Remained in position all day – "C" "D" Coys. relieved by South African Infantry at 2400. Relief completed by 0330. 12th.	J.E.
"		1100	Marched back to PEVMONT and billeted.	J.E.
"			Marched to MAUROIS and billeted. Total casualties during operations 10 Officers 265 O.Rs. Total capture by Battalion 1 gun intact, 2 " damaged, 9 Anti-Tank guns, 6 M.G.s. 150 prisoners.	J.E.
MAUROIS	13	0900	Marched to MARETZ and billeted. "B" Team rejoins Bn.	J.E.
MARETZ	14		Rest, reorganizing. Remained at MARETZ.	J.E.
"	15		Battalion marched to PEVMONT at 1020. 1700 moved up to line relieved Gloucesters. "D" Coy relieved 1 Coy South African. Bn HQrs K.32.b.0.9.	J.E.
K.32.b.0.9.	16	0400	Bn HQrs moved to K.27.c.4.8 where they kept the day they	J.E.

WAR DIARY
or
INTELLIGENCE SUMMARY.
(Erase heading not required.)

Army Form C. 2118.

Place	Date	Hour	Summary of Events and Information	Remarks and references to Appendices
			were heavily shelled with H.E. & Yellow Cross – 0800 'A'&'D' Coys were ordered to assist 6 RDF in anything to Rly bridge (TP5) Battalion Orders received to proceed forthwith LE CATEAU – 1720 opened of 1835 crossing R. SELLE at TP.4.c.2.2 by free return Bridge. 'B' & 'C' Coys bridged Rly cutting at TP.a.3.2 + 4 P.m. 'A'&'D' Coys crossed gauge line at TP.5.a.2.5.	M.S.
Q.2.ce.2.d	18.		Battalion remained at Q.2 central throughout day. A few heavy calibre shells fell recently we for flying about way.	M.S.
"	19.		Enemy Rly A.A. Anti-Aircraft Gun. Some hostile heavily shelled at 19.20 hrs. orders received to push and stand tonight in conjunction with 13th 90th W.Y. & 9th Manchester Regt. 'A'&'D' Coys detailed for this duty Orders cancelled shortly after & 'A'&'D' recalled.	
"	20	0100	Relieved by 6th Lancs. Fus. (Hqrs remained in same position) B.T.G. Coys heavily shelled & line with H.E. Yper. shells.	M.S.
		1845	Bn. relieved marched to MAURIS billeted arriving about 2300	
MAUROIS	21	1030	Parade starting point on route to PREMONT arrived & billeted at 1245	5.S.

Army Form C. 2118.

WAR DIARY
or
INTELLIGENCE SUMMARY.
(Erase heading not required.)

Instructions regarding War Diaries and Intelligence Summaries are contained in F.S. Regs., Part II. and the Staff Manual respectively. Title pages will be prepared in manuscript.

Place	Date	Hour	Summary of Events and Information	Remarks and references to Appendices
PREMONT	22		Coys. noted, relieving up, Bath etc. Tank demonstration afternoon	
"	23		Ch. Prad. (R.C.P.) infection. L.G. classes started. Baths	
"	24		Inspection v. L.G. classes. Training continued	
"	25		Route March 10 miles - clean fatigue dress	
"	26		"	
"	27		Divine Services	
"	28		Brigade Route March in "Battle Order" dress - return detour. 10 miles - 2 am fall out	
"	29		Companies at disposal of Coy Commdrs. for musketry arm drill etc. in morning, Gas demonstration by Divisional Gas Officer	

WAR DIARY
or
INTELLIGENCE SUMMARY.

Army Form C. 2118.

Place	Date	Hour	Summary of Events and Information	Remarks and references to Appendices
PREMONT	30	8:30	Battalion paraded & marched to X13 d.4 - deemed a route getting into Artillery formation quickly - changing front & attacking sty point -	W/2
"	31		① Internal Field day - Special Idea - "Our advance resisted general line - ESNES - WALINCOURT - SERAIN - PREMONT - BOHAIN GUISE Road by midday" - Battalion formed up immediately in rear of the WALINCOURT - SERAIN Road & attacked at 1700 Ant snipped up FELINCOURT and BOIS DE PINON, - being relieved by A Coy 1st West 6th R.D.F. in support, passed through Venture the attack - Operation ceased at 16.30. Battalion marched back to PREMONT.	

3/10/18

J.S. Colum Lt Col
Comdg 5th R.Innis.Fus.

190TH INFANTRY BRIGADE.

Brigade Commander.   Brigadier General A.J. HUNTER, D.S.O., MC.
Brigade Major.   Captain R.A. EDEN, M.C.
Staff Captain.   Captain P. INGLESON, M.C.
Brigade Intell. Offr.   Captain T.H.G. GREY, M.C.
Brigade Signalling Offr. Lieut. A.T. TERRY.

6th LANCASHIRE FUSILIERS.

Commanding Officer.   Lieut. Colonel R.F. GROSS, D.S.O.
Second-in-Command.   Major J.S. TOWNSHEND, M.C.
Adjutant.   Captain F. FRANKS, M.C.

O.C., "A" Coy.   Captain R.A.V. WHITE.
O.C., "B" Coy.   Captain J.S. RUTHERFORD.
O.C., "C" Coy.   Captain L.B.L. BECKHAM, M.C.
O.C., "D" Coy.   Captain C.H. POTTER, M.C.

5TH R. INNISKILLING FUS.

Commanding Officer.   Lieut. Colonel A.W.B. PATERSON, D.S.O.
Second-in-Command.   Major G.M. KIDD, M.C.
Adjutant.   Captain H.J. EASTWOOD, M.C.

O.C., "A" Coy.   Captain G.R. ROCHE-KELLY.
O.C., "B" Coy.   Captain W.C.G. BOLITHO.
O.C., "C" Coy.   Captain W.R. GALLWAY.
O.C., "D" Coy.   Captain T.T.H. VERSCHOYLE.

6TH R. DUBLIN FUSILIERS.

Commanding Officer.   Lieut. Colonel W.B. LITTLE, D.S.O., M.C.
Second-in-Command.   Major W. VANCE, M.C.
Adjutant.   Captain J. ESMONDE, M.C.

O.C., "A" Coy.   Captain H.J. HOYE.
O.C., "B" Coy.   Captain H.A. SHADFORTH.
O.C., "C" Coy.   Captain H.J. GAFFNEY, M.C.
O.C., "D" Coy.   Captain W.B. ENGLISH.

190TH L.T.M.B.

Officer Commanding.   A/Captain F.J. ROE.

198TH INFANTRY BRIGADE.

REPORT ON OPERATIONS.

7.10.18 - 12.10.18.

----:----

PART I.

7.10.18 - 18.00 8.10.18.

----:----

1. ASSEMBLY.

On 7th October the 198th Infantry Brigade Group moved by march route to the vicinity of LE CATELET and occupied their assembly position in the LE CATELET - NAUROY line.

Battalions were distributed as follows :-

    5th R. Inniskilling Fus. RIGHT.
    6th R. Dublin Fus.   LEFT.
    5th Lancs. Fus.   RESERVE, in the
                               GOUY - BELLICOURT
                               railway cutting.

198th Infantry Brigade H.Q. RAILWAY RIDGE.

2. DEPLOYMENT.

On the evening of 7th October units began their march to position of deployment at 23.00. Rain began about 19.00 and fell heavily till 22.00. The 'going' was as a result very slippery. In spite of this all units moved forward very well and were approaching their tapes in good time.

At 01.00 an attack on VILLERS OUTREAUX resulted in a heavy hostile barrage being put down on our positions of deployment.

The 6th R. Dublin Fus. were lining up on their tapes and the 5th R. Inniskilling Fus. were just nearing them when the barrage came down.

Both battalions suffered considerable casualties and were correspondingly disorganised.

/Heavy shelling continued

Heavy shelling continued throughout the period of deployment.

At 04.45 however, both battalions were in position on their tapes ready to advance.

The 6th Bn. Lancashire Fus. had meanwhile assembled in Reserve without much difficulty.

One Section of 198th L.T.M.B. was allotted to each Battalion, and the guns with 28 rounds of ammunition were brought up on pack mules and off loaded at the positions of deployment.

3. ATTACK.

At 05.10 our barrage opened and the infantry advanced to the attack.

On the whole the enemy showed little tendency to fight, and often ran away before our troops could get to grips with him, with the exception of M.G. nests which fought stoutly.

From the earliest stages of the attack the 6th R. Dublin Fus. were troubled by machine gun fire on their left flank.

As the attack progressed this became more serious as VILLERS OUTREAUX was not taken and the enemy had therefore a perfect target for enfilade M.G. fire. In spite of these difficulties the 6th R. Dublin Fus. pushed on and captured PETIT VERGER Farm and MARLICHES Farm. The latter they were unable to hold owing to enfilade M.G. fire.

The 6th R. Dublin Fus. then established a defensive flank along the ridge in T.29.b. This flank was further extended by four posts which were established by the 6th Bn. Lancashire Fus. in T.29.c.

On the right the 5th R. Inniskilling Fus. continued their advance and established themselves on the RED LINE.

There was some fighting in HANTGE FARM and HANTGE WOOD but, with the assistance of tanks, the wood was soon cleared and a battery of 77 mm. was captured.

/The position at 09.15

The position at 08.15 was approximately as shown on attached map. (Map A. position 2)

At 08.45 the enemy counter attacked N. of HAMAGE FARM. This counter attack was repulsed with the assistance of two tanks.

During the next hour there were several minor actions along the MALINCOURT - AUDIGNY Line, the enemy attempting to debouch from there to counter attack our troops establishing themselves on the RED LINE. All these local counter attacks were repulsed with loss to the enemy.

At 10.30 the 6th R. Dublin Fus. established touch with the battalion on their left the 4th K.R.R.C. of the 50th Division.

As our troops advanced along the S.E. side of VILLERS OUTREAUX the 6th R. Dublin Fus. advanced again and captured MARLICHES FARM (11.30) and established themselves along the line of their final objective (Green Line on attached Map "A"). At the same time the 5th R. Innis. Fus. continued their advance, captured LAMPE FARM, and established themselves on the Green Line. (Map A position 3)

PART II.

18.00 8.10.18 - 18.00 9.10.18.

---:---

1. RELIEF OF PORTION OF 199th Infantry Brigade FRONT.

About 17.00 on 8th October orders were received from the Divisional Commander that the Brigade would take over a portion of the front of 199th Infantry Brigade who were carrying out a minor operation with a view to re-adjusting their front before an attack the next morning.

Unfortunately G.O.C., 199th Infantry Brigade and his Brigade Major were both in the line arranging for this minor operation, and details for relief could not be arranged till 19.00. It was then decided that the 5th R. Innis. Fus. should relieve the 9th Manchester Regt., less 1 Coy. in U.7.central and LAMPE POST to be relieved by 6th R. Dublin Fus.

which was

The latter portion of the relief was carried out, but owing to a misunderstanding the three Coys., 9th Manchester Regt., were not relieved by 5th R. Inniskilling Fus. (see map B position 4

2. ORDERS FOR ATTACK ON 9TH OCTOBER.

About 00.15 on 9th October orders were received for an attack the next morning.

It was decided that the 6th Lancs. Fus. would lead the attack with 5th R. Inniskilling Fus. in Support and 6th R. Dublin Fus. in Reserve.

3. ATTACK.

6th Lancs. Fus. were formed up at 04.50 and advanced at 05.20 clearing the eastern outskirts of ELINCOURT.

Two Coys. of 5th R. Inniskilling Fus. followed up and entered ELINCOURT from the South and East. The remaining Companies were late reaching their assembly position.

It soon became evident that the enemy had withdrawn and would offer no serious resistance in ELINCOURT.

/The 6th R. Dublin Fus. entered

The 6th R. Dublin Fus. entered the village from the West and with the assistance of the 5th R. Inniskilling Fus. rapidly cleared the village capturing some dozen prisoners. (see map B. position 5)

A section of R.E. were detailed to search for booby traps and mines in ELINCOURT.

They discovered an unexploded charge under the Railway Crossing at the Southern exit of the village.

Considerable delay was caused by a very dense fog which lasted from 06.00 to 07.15 when the 6th Lancs. Fus. continued their advance without meeting any organized opposition, captured the BOIS DE PINON and IRIS COPSE and reached their final objective - the M'METZ-CL'RY Road at 10.50, sending patrols to S. exit of CL'RY to gain touch with Brigade on our left. (see map B. position 6)

The 5th R. Inniskilling Fus. then moved up into Support sending one Company to IRIS F'RM to secure their left flank, and the 6th R. Dublin Fus. into Reserve.

The South African Brigade who had been following up close in rear of the Brigade then passed through the 6th Lancs. Fus. and continued the advance.

At 12.00 the Brigade was therefore distributed in accordance with attached map "B".

4. BRIGADE IN DIVISIONAL RESERVE.

Orders were received at 13.00 that the Brigade was in Divisional Reserve and would hold the RED LINE (final objective of 198 and 199 Infantry Brigades) in the event of a hostile counter attack.

All units were ordered to be prepared to move at 2 hours notice, and O.C., "A" Coy., 25th M.G. Battalion was ordered to place eight guns in position covering the southern portion of the Red Line in addition to the eight already in position in the Northern Sub-sector. (map B. position 7)

PART III.

18.00 9.10.18 - 05.00 11.10.18.

----:----

1. ORDERS FOR ATTACK.

At 00.30 the Divisional Commander dictated to the G.O.C. on the telephone orders for attack at 06.00 10th October.

2. APPROACH MARCH.

At 03.30 10th October the Brigade marched through MARETZ and MAUROIS to REUMONT.

3. ADVANCE.

East of REUMONT the Brigade deployed at 06.15 N. of REUMONT - LE CATEAU Road. The advance was carried out on a one battalion front with three Companies in the line.

The 6th Lancs. Fus. again led the attack with the 5th R. Inniskilling Fus. in Support and the 6th R. Dublin Fus. in Reserve.

Touch was obtained with 199th Infantry Brigade on the right, and with the 2nd Argyle and Sutherland Highlanders of the 33rd Division on the left. 199th Infantry Brigade were deployed before this Brigade as they led the march to the position of deployment. 199th Infantry Brigade accordingly advanced slowly in order to allow this Brigade to get into line with them.

Owing to the very short time available in which to make arrangements for this attack it was impossible to arrange for artillery co-operation.

The Brigade advanced accordingly without artillery Support.

At the outset of the attack little opposition was encountered either from hostile shell or machine gun fire, but as our troops neared LE CATEAU the shelling became heavy.

The enemy had evidently several batteries, chiefly 5.9, ready in position, and the 6th Lancs. Fus. in particular suffered casualties from shell fire.

/77 mm. firing over open sights

-2-

77 mm. firing over open sights on the forward slopes in K.21 and K.27 were particularly troublesome.

In spite of these difficulties the 6th Lancs. Fus. pushed on and captured the high ground in K.27.b. and d.

The high ground and the line of the INCHY - LE CATEAU Railway were very heavily shelled and it became evident that a further advance without more artillery support and without counter-battery work would be difficult.

The enemy was holding the line of the River SELLE in strength.

The situation at 12.00 was as shown on attached map "C".

4. ATTACK ON MONTAY.

At 16.25 verbal orders were received by the G.O.C. from the Divisional Commander that the Brigade would attack and capture MONTAY at 17.00.

This order was communicated verbally to O.C., 6th Lancashire Fus. by the Brigade Major at 16.45 and at 17.30 the 6th Lancs. Fus. advanced on MONTAY.

The advance came under heavy machine gun fire from the Eastern bank of the river.

In spite of this the 6th Lancs. Fus. pressed on and entered MONTAY supported by two Coys. 5th R. Inniskilling Fus.

Touch was established with 18th K.L. on the right but it was found impossible to cross the river as the bridges were broken and the river was unfordable. (22.55).

Our line then ran as shown on attached map "D".

5. Throughout the 11th the situation remained approximately unchanged. Some casualties were suffered from the enemy's shell fire which was still very heavy.

Arrangements were made for the relief of the 6th Lancs. Fus. and the 6th R. Dublin Fus. during the night 11th/12th and instructions were given to

/O.C., 6th R. Dublin Fus.

O.C., 6th R. Dublin Fus. to endeavour to cross the river SELLE, and get into touch with troops of the 33rd Division on the high ground East of the river.

At 17.00 orders were received that the Brigade would be relieved that night by a portion of the South African Brigade.

The relief was effected without incident, though the shell fire was heavy, and the Brigade concentrated in billets in REUMONT.

To sum up the Brigade were in action practically continuously from dawn 8th Oct. to dawn 12th Oct. During this period the Brigade advanced 13 miles, 9 miles of which were realised fighting.

28 guns and a number of prisoners were captured and two villages were liberated.

Total captures made during this period were :-

77mm. Guns.	5.9" How.	Anti-Tank Rifles.	T.Ms.	A.A. Guns.	M.Gs. counted.
23	3	3	2	1	48.

Prisoners - 342 O.R.

Total casualties during this period were :-

Officers.		O.R.			
K.	W.	K.	W.	NYD.	M.
4	26	71	579	1	125 ⊗

⊗ Practically all these have been accounted for, either K, W, or M., i.e.,

K.	W.	M?
13.	59	53x.

x. All these 53 must be either killed or wounded in our hands. No men fell into enemy hands as far as is known.

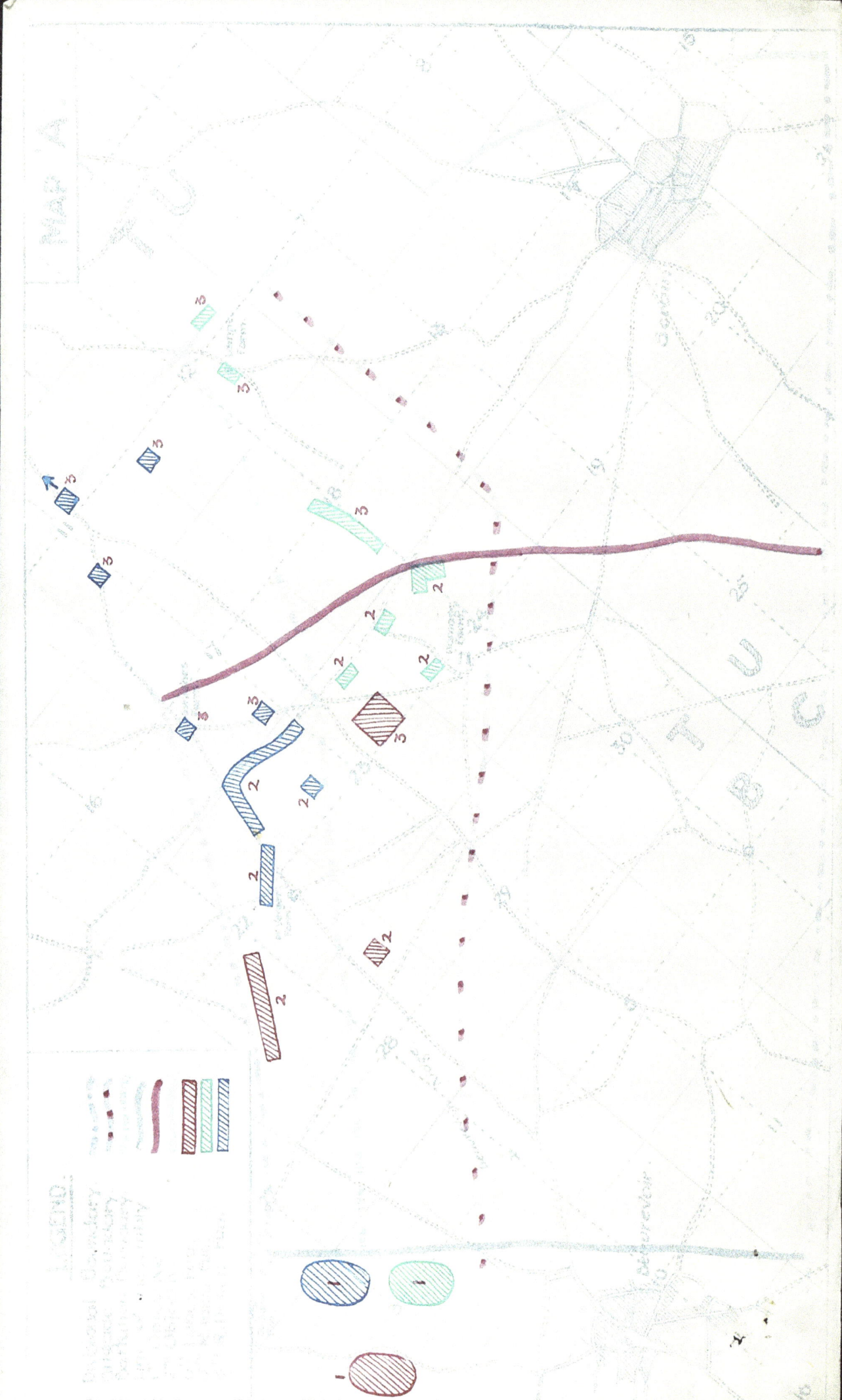

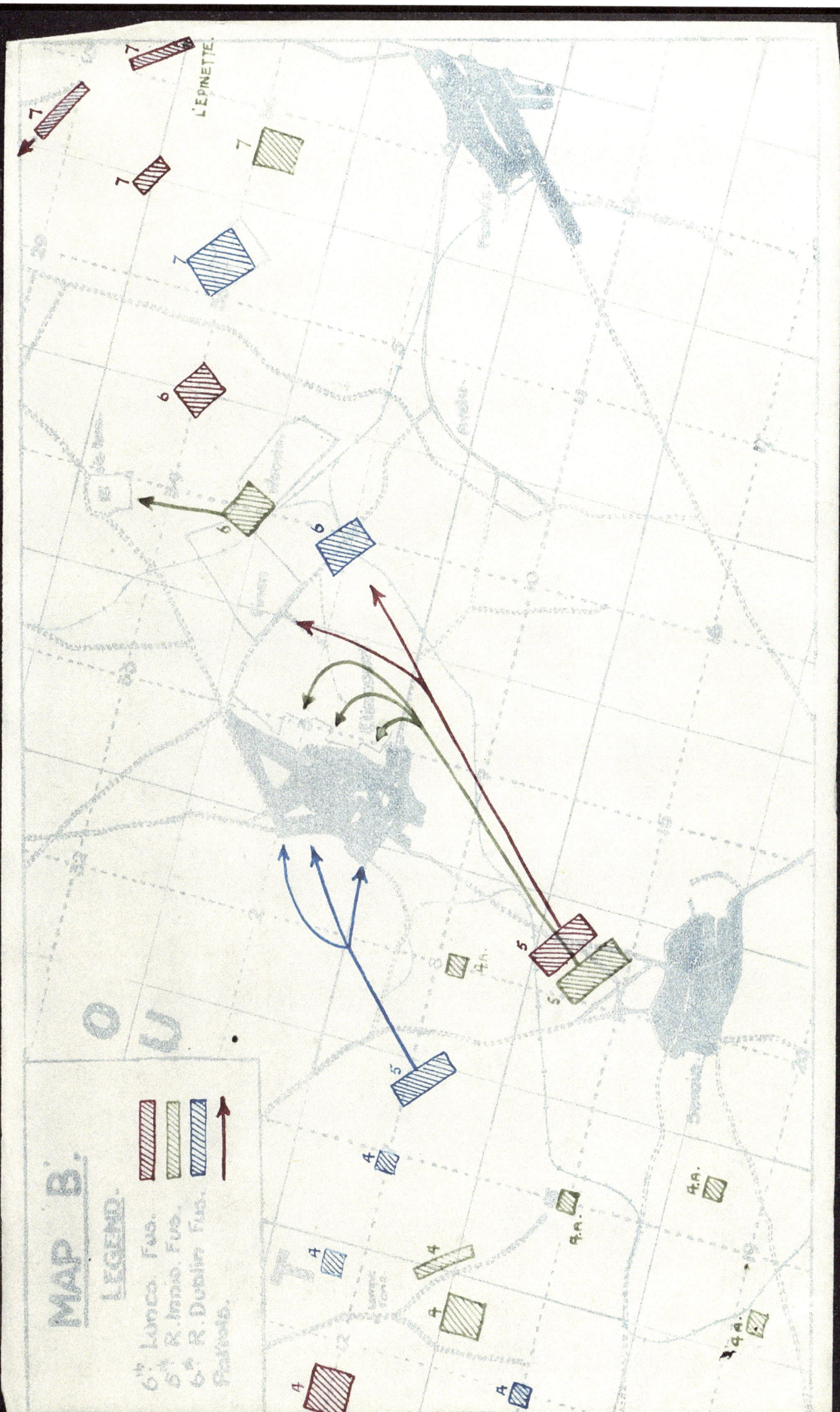

MAP 'C'.

LEGEND.

6ᵗʰ Lancs. Fus.
5ᵗʰ R Innis. Fus.
6ᵗʰ R Dublin Fus.

MAP 'D'

LEGEND.

6ᵗʰ Lancs. Fus.
5ᵗʰ R. Innis. Fus.
5ᵗʰ R. Dublin Fus.

1:20000

Parts of {57ᵈᵉ ᴺᴱ / 57ᵈᵉ ˢᴱ}

LE CATEAU
Montay
Troisvilles

ACCOUNT OF OPERATIONS.

PART IV.

12th October, 1918 - 12.00 18th October, 1918.

THE CLEARING OF LE CATEAU.

-:-:-:-:-

PART V.

12.00 18th October - 18.00 18th October, 1918

THE ADVANCE TO THE RED LINE.

-:-:-:-:-

PART VI.

18.00 18th October, 1918 - 20th October, 1918.

PATROLS AND RELIEF.

-:-:-:-:-

PART IV.

12th October, 1918 - 12.00 18th October, 1918.

-:-:-:-:-:-

After the relief by South African Brigade, described in Part III, the 198th Infantry Brigade went into Divisional Reserve :- first at REUMONT at 2 hours notice, then at MAUROIS and finally at MARETZ where the Brigade was settled in Billets at 14.00 on 13th October.

The Brigade remained at MARETZ till the morning of the 16th when it moved to REUMONT. Later in the day it moved again and took up positions as follows :-

Unit.	Position.	In relief of.	Remarks.
Brigade H.Q.	Q.7.a.	S.A. Brigade H.Q.	
1 Coy., R. Innis. Fus.	Q.3 & Q.6.	S.A. Brigade.	
R. Dub. Fus. less 2 Cos.	W. of LE CATEAU.	S.A. Brigade.	Front Line posts.

/2 Cos., R. Dub. Fus.

2 Cos., 6 R.Dub.Fus.	Q.2.central.	–	For clearing LE CATEAU from the N. & N.E. & E.
5 R.Innis.Fus. less 2 Cos.	Roman Road to N.W.end of MONTAY.	9 Glouc. Regt.	Front Line posts.
1 Co., 5 R.Innis.Fus.	Q.7.	–	Brigade Reserve.
Lancs. Fus.	Q.7.	–	Divl. Reserve.
190 L.T.M.B.	With R.Dub.Fus.		For clearing LE CATEAU.

On conclusion of relief, the S.A. Brigade concentrated in the ravines in K.26 and 27 preparatory to forcing the crossing of the SELLE and taking the Red Line K.36.d.c.5 to BAILLON FARM, with a defensive flank to the North.

The two Companies 6th R. Dublin Fus. were to follow close behind them and start mopping up LE CATEAU from the N.E. and E. – when they had made some progress the remainder of 6 R. Dublin Fus. were to press in from the West and finally the Eastern outskirts of the town were to be put in a state of defence.

The 50th Divn. on our right were to take the red dotted line which included the Railway Station and the triangle in Q.5 before the S.A. attack and the mopping up of LE CATEAU were to begin. On their reaching this line the Coy. of 5th R. Innis. Fus. in Q.3 and Q.9 would be unnecessary and the plan was for them and the Coy. in Brigade Reserve to move up and take the place of the Dublins W. of LE CATEAU.

In spite of the 50th Division not getting either the station or triangle, the S.A. attack was launched and the mopping-up Companies of the Dublins were put in. They had considerable difficulty in their task and first one and then the other Company of 5th R. Innis. Fus. were sent up to 6th R. Dublin Fus. so as to release more men of the Dublins for the mopping up of the town – which was urgent as S.A. Brigade were being much troubled by M.G. fire and small counter attacks along the railway

/from the road crossing

from the road crossing K.35.c.9.3 northwards.
Messages were received from Division authorising the
employment of all the Dublins in this mopping up
(the force had been limited to two Companies at the
outset) and eventually all the Dublins and a platoon
or two of Inniskillings were employed.

At 10.40 a telephone message from the Divisional
Commander placed 6th Lancs. Fus. at Brigade disposal
with instructions that as 50th Division had taken the
station and triangle,   6th Lancs. Fus. were to cross
the R. SELLE at ST. BENIN or north of it and attack
the objective - road crossing K.35.c.9.3. to
K.35.c.0.5 - with the idea of completing the clearing
of LE CATEAU promptly.

The Battalion was therefore sent off, and
succeeded in passing two companies across the river
at Mins. de Pont Chapelle in Q.9.b.   The station
and railway triangle which dominate the valley
entirely were not in our hands.   This was reported
by 6th Lancs. Fus. and eventually instructions were
received from Division to withdraw them again into
Divisional Reserve.   This was done and completed at
14.00 at the cost of some dozen casualties and a
certain amount of fatigue to the battalion.

The mopping up of LE CATEAU was going on slowly
in the mean-time and section after section of the
town was reported in our hands,- till the whole of
the main town was ours at 17.50 the Faubourg de
Landrecies being however still distinctly German,
and commanded from the Railway Triangle and the
embankment and crossing at K.35.c.9.3.

Throughout the night the situation on our right
at the Railway Triangle and the Station was obscure.
Notification was received of an attack being in
preparation to capture these two points by the
division on our right but this attack was postponed.
Under instructions from Division orders were therefore
issued at 23.45 to the 6th Lancs. Fus. (who were
placed at the disposal of G.O.C. at this time and
ceased to be in Divisional Reserve) to get into touch
with the 6th R. Dublin Fus. and reconnoitre with a

/view to

view to

(a) Taking over the line from the 6th R. Dublin Fus. and establishing their line from K.35.central – Road and railway crossing K.35.c.9.3 – C.4.b.3.1 – River with advanced posts pushed forward to road junction K.35.d.6.0.

(b) To assemble on approximate front K.35.central – K.35.c.7.0 for an attack on the objective K.36.d.3.7 – Cross Roads K.36.a.00 95.

The task (b) was only to be undertaken in the event of the capture of the railway triangle by the Division on our right.

At 00.50 on the 18th orders were issued for Task (a) to be carried out. During the night and previous to relief the 6th R. Dublin Fus. completed the mopping up of the FAUBOURG de LANDRECIES except that the railway crossing at K.35.c.9.3 could not be captured as long as the enemy held Railway Triangle.

Touch was obtained with the South African Brigade on the railway in K.35.central.

The relief of 6th R. Dublin Fus. by the 6th Lancs. Fus. in LE CATEAU proved very difficult to carry out. The enemy shelled the West end of the town throughout the night with a large proportion of gas shell of all kinds, and the difficulties of relieving posts and patrols scattered all over the town were very great. A mist added to the difficulties of relief. In spite of this the relief was complete shortly after 09.00.

Meanwhile the Division on our right attacked at dawn and captured the Railway Triangle about 06.30.

The 6th Lancs. Fus. immediately got into touch with the 13th Black Watch on their right who carried out this attack and pushed forward and seized the road and railway crossing at K.35.c.9.3.

This position was an extremely strong one and owing to the Railway Triangle not having been captured had resisted all our efforts to capture it throughout the 17th.

At 10.00 on the 18th the Brigade was therefore disposed as follows :-

6th Lancs. Fus.

Two Companies in depth along line of Railway from K.35.central where in touch with S.A. Brigade - K.35.c.9.0.

One Company in close Support in Eastern outskirts of LE CATEAU.

One Company in Reserve near Battalion H.Q. at K.33.b.5.4.

5th R. Inniskilling Fus.

In support in Q.2.

6th R. Dublin Fus.

In Brigade Reserve in Q.7.

198th L.T.M.B. was attached to the 6th R. Dublin Fus. to assist in the mopping up of LE CATEAU.

2 Guns were attached to the 2 Companies of 6th R.D.F. who worked round from the N. and N.E., and 2 Guns to the 2 Companies that worked into LE CATEAU from the West.

They were of considerable assistance in dealing with hostile M.G. posts in houses in LE CATEAU.

About 100 rounds were fired in all during the 17th, and 18th instant.

The total casualties sustained by the 6th R.Dub.Fus. during the mopping up of LE CATEAU, were :-
Killed - 13.
Wounded - 64 (including 3 at duty)
Missing - 9.

Captures during this action were :-

	Prisoners.	Lorries.	M.G's.
6 R. Dub.Fus.	95	3	? x
6 Lancs.Fus.	12	-	-
5 Innis. Fus.	-	-	2

x All material found in LE CATEAU is claimed and this includes many more M.G's, the number of which it is impossible to estimate.

PART V.

The Advance to the RED LINE.

12.00, 18th October to 18.00, 18th October, 1918.

-:-:-:-:-:-:-:-:-

After the capture of the line of the Railway, the 6th Lancs.Fus. pushed towards the RED Line and at 16.30 held the following line with three Companies in depth:-
K.36.c.3.3. - K.35.b.5.5.
One Company and Battalion H.Q., at K.35.d.4.4.

On reaching this line the 6th Lancs.Fus. came under hostile machine gun fire. The Battalion accordingly halted for 45 minutes while arrangements were made for the co-operation of troops of the 25th Division on the Right for the final advance to the RED Line. This halt of 45 minutes also enabled the advance to be continued at dusk.

At 17.15 the advance was resumed and was very successful. The bad light hampered the enemy Machine Gunners, prisoners from whom afterwards stated that they were unable to see our men until they were right up to them.
The RED Line was reached from K.36.d.0.6. - K.36.a.0.9., 5 Machine Guns and 35 prisoners were captured, and severe casualties were inflicted on the enemy.

This engagement furnished an interesting instance of the vulnerability of hostile machine guns against infantry employing their own weapons skillfully and making the best use of ground.
More enemy could undoubtedly have been killed and captured had any Cavalry or fresh Infantry been available to exploit the success. Large numbers of enemy and some transport were seen retreating hurriedly eastwards.

The 6th Lancs.Fus. then consolidated the RED Line and pushed forward patrols towards RICHEMONT River. These patrols soon got into touch with more hostile Machine Guns

/ The 5th R.Innis.Fus

The 5th R.Innis.Fus. ~~pushed~~ moved up on to RAILWAY TRIANGLE (Q.5.) at 18.00 to be in Support to the 6th Lancs.Fus.

From the time of their relief of 6th R.Dublin Fus. until the capture of the RED Line, on the evening of the 18th, the 6th Lancs.Fus. captured 5 Machine Guns, and 47 prisoners (25 of whom were captured in the final advance to the RED Line).

In the same period they suffered the following casualties :-

      Killed   -   4 O.R.
      Wounded -   16 O.R.

PART VI.

18.00 18th October, 1918 - 20th October, 1918.

-:-:-:-:-:-

Under instructions received from Division, orders were issued to the 6th Lancs. Fus. at 16.15 on 18th October to re-adjust their front as follows :-

(a) To hand over the Red Line from K.36.central to K.36.a.0.0 to the 9th Manchester Regt. Relief to be complete as soon as possible after dusk.

(b) To take over the Red Line from K.36.central to Q.6.b.6.0 from 13th Black Watch (Scottish Horse) of 50th Division, as soon as the latter were definitely in possession of that portion of the Red Line.

The relief of 6th Lancs. Fus. by 9th Manchester Regt. was not complete until 02.00 on the 19th instant. In the meantime reports had been received from the 149th Infantry Brigade that the 13th Black Watch were not on the Red Line.

Orders were accordingly sent to the 6th Lancs. Fus. to side slip to their right on relief by 9th Manchester Regt. and establish themselves as far as possible on the Red Line from K.36.central to Q.6.b.6.0.

On reconnoitring to carry out this order 6th Lancs. Fus. found troops of the Gloucesters of the 25th Division on this portion of the Red Line.

As the Red Line was held throughout its length
and relief by 8th Manchester Regt. could not be
completed till very late at night O.C., 8th Lancs.
Fus. decided to concentrate his Battalion about
K.35.d.1.4. and carry out the relief of whoever was
holding his portion of the Red Line as soon as
possible after daylight.   While 6th Lancs. Fus.
were concentrating the Gloucesters of the 25th
Division were withdrawn and the 13th Black Watch
took over a portion only of the front establishing a
post on the North side of the LE CATEAU - BAZUEL
road about Q.6.b.2.2.

The 8th Manchester Regt. filled this gap by
placing a post about Q.6.b.3.9.

Shortly after daylight 6th Lancs. Fus. took
over their sector of the Red Line from the road at
Q.6.b.5.0 where they were in touch with the 13th
Black Watch to K.36.d.0.6. where they were in touch
with 8th Manchester Regt.

The morning of the 19th instant was very quiet.
There was practically no hostile artillery fire. Some
hostile machine guns were active from about the line
of road K.36.d.9.2 - K.36.d.8.9.

Arrangements were then made for 5th R. Inniskilling
Fus. to push out strong patrols to the RICHEMONT
River at dusk and to secure the line of the river
as outpost line from the Mill at R.2.a.1.5 to GARDE
MILL (L.31.a.90.85).

One Battery of 63rd Brigade, R.F.A. was detailed
to assist 5th R. Innis. Fus. in their   to
the outpost line, and a liaison officer for this
purpose reported to this Battalion.

Verbal orders were received from Division at
22.00 on 18th instant that the advance to the line of
the RICHEMONT River would be carried out under an
artillery barrage at 07.00 on 20th instant in
conjunction with an advance by 18 Infantry Brigade.
Orders were accordingly issued to 5th R. Innis. Fus.
to report by 03.00 on the 20th the position of their
patrols.   If no report was received by that hour
patrols would have to withdraw to the Red Line and
advance under cover of the barrage at 07.00 in
conjunction with 18 Infantry Brigade.   There is

/little doubt

little doubt that patrols of 5th R. Inniskilling Fus. would have reached the line of the RICHEMONT river solely by the use of infantry weapons and without the assistance of an artillery barrage as the enemy had only a few machine gun posts along the line of the road K.36.d.2.2 - K.36.d.8.2. These were not dug in and could be enfiladed from the road at Q.6.b.6.0. Arrangements had already been made for enfilade fire to be brought to bear on them from a post at this point.

At 23.30 on the 19th instant verbal instructions were received from the Divisional Commander that the 14th Infantry Brigade would take over the front held by this Brigade at once from the Northern Brigade Boundary to K.36.d.6.0., and that the Southern portion of the Brigade front would be taken over at once by 25th Division.

The advance to the RICHEMONT River would be carried out by 14th Infantry Brigade on the whole Divisional front.

Patrols of 5th R. Inniskilling Fus. were accordingly withdrawn at once.

In order to enable the 6th Lancs. Fus. to be withdrawn without delay, the 5th R. Inniskilling Fus. (less two Companies) were instructed to take over the Southern portion of the Brigade front pending relief by the 25th Division.

6th Lancs. Fus. were relieved in the northern portion of the Brigade front by the 5th Manchester Regt, and the whole battalion was concentrated by 07.00 on 20th October in Q.7.

6th R. Dublin Fus. meanwhile moved from Q.2. to REUMONT and 2 Coys. 5th R. Innis. Fus. moved to Q.8.

The whole of the Brigade was thus relieved by 03.30 on 20th October except the 5th R. Innis. Fus. (less two Companies) who were awaiting relief by troops of the 25th Division.

This relief was considerably delayed and when finally arrangements were made for 20th Manchesters to carry out this relief the battalion reported that the relief could not be carried out until dusk owing to hostile machine gun fire.

/Relief accordingly took place

-4-

Relief accordingly took place at dusk on 20th October and the 5th R. Inniskilling Fus. (less two Companies) reached MAUROIS at 22.30 on 20th instant.

The remainder of the Brigade marched to MAUROIS on the afternoon of the 20th instant.

The following are the casualties sustained by this Brigade from the 18th October to 20th October, both dates inclusive :-

	Officers.			O.R.		
	K.	W.	M.	K.	W.	M.
6th Lancs. Fus.	-	1	-	4	68 x	2.
5th Innis.Fus.	-	1	-	-	20 ø	8
6th R.D.F.	1	3	-	12	61 ø	9
	1	5	-	16	128	19.

ø Includes 3 at duty.
x   "   6 " "

TOTAL CAPTURES (from 18th to 20th inst.)

Prisoners.	Lorries.	M.G's.
107.	3	2 x

x All material found in LE CATEAU is claimed and this includes many more M.G's, the numbers of which it is impossible to estimate.

SPECIAL ORDER.
----

1.   I wish heartily to congratulate all ranks of all arms and departments of the Division on the result of their first appearance on the Battle Field after their reorganisation as the 66th Division.

The operations between October 8th and October 19th which were in many respects as unique as they were successful may be summarised as follows :-

8th Oct.   After a successful frontal attack at 05.00 by the S.A. Bde and 198th Bde on a first objective 3,800 yards in depth and 3,800 yards in width, 199th Bde went through and exploited the situation on the same frontage to a depth of a further 2,300 yards, finally capturing the village of SERAIN by 19.00.

9th Oct.   During the night 8th/9th the Divisional front was reorganised and at 05.00 October 9th the pursuit was continued by 199th Bde on Right, 198th Bde on Left, and S.A. Bde in Reserve, each Bde advancing on a front of 1,500 yards narrowing to 1000 yards on the first objective, which was 5,000 yards distant. This objective was secured at 10.45. At 11.00 South African Bde passed through to continue the pursuit for a further 4,500 yards to a second objective which was secured about 14.00. Cavalry then passed through and held a line covering REUMONT and TROISVILLES. During the night the South African Bde threw out an outpost line astride the ROMAN ROAD in relief of the Cavalry immediately N.E. of REUMONT.

10th Oct.   At 05.00 199th Bde on the Right and 198th Bde on the Left, each on a 1,000 yards front, passed through the South African Bde outpost line and took up the pursuit.

MONTAY and that portion of LE CATEAU West of the River SELLE, was secured by 10.00.

The Division had advanced 14 miles on a two mile front in 53 hours, taking many villages and ending up with LE CATEAU.

Prisoners were taken from eight Divisions, viz :- 2nd Guards, 8th Division, 21st Division, 21st Reserve Division, 38th Division, 119th Division, 121st Division, and 204th Division, also from 75th M.G. Marksman Detachment and from 4th Saxon Cyclist Brigade.

26 Officers (including 3 Battalion Commanders) and 1031 O.R. had been captured and also following materiel :- 62 ·77 guns and 4.2" Hows., 3 8" Hows., 3 5.9" How., 1 Anti-Aircraft gun, 15 T.Ms., 6 Anti-tank Rifles, 126 M.Gs. and 2 Motor cars.

Patrols were pushed into and had occupied the greater part of LE CATEAU East of the River by 10.00.

At 17.30 5th Bn Connaught Rangers rushed the town and secured a footing on the railway embankment East of the town, killing many enemy.

From conversation with the Mayor of LE CATEAU, it appears that the confusion and panic in the town was very great. A few dead of the Connaught Rangers were afterwards found on the high ground N.E. of the railway embankment about the RED Line of the attack on the 17th. Owing to the high ground on either flank remaining in the enemy's hands, we were however forced to withdraw.

/11th Oct....

- 2 -

11th Oct.	On the night 11th/12th the S.A. Bde took over the Divisional front, less that portion north of the ROMAN ROAD which was relieved by the 9th Bn Glouc. R.
12th Oct. to 17th Oct.	On 12th October to October 17th the S.A. Bde prepared for the attack on the high ground N.E. of LE CATEAU. The 17th Reserve Division had come into the line opposite the Division after seven weeks rest on the night 10th/11th Oct. and at once proceeded to organise the position E. of the River and the Eastern part of the town, even pushing patrols across to the Western bank.
17th Oct.	At 05.20 the 50th Division, in conjunction with the rest of the Fourth Army, attacked on our Right. At this hour the South African Bde was assembled in its jumping off position N. of LE CATEAU, on the eastern bank of River SELLE having crossed by means of eight 30 foot bridges made and placed in position by the Divisional Engineers. The Brigade attacked at 08.05 having been covered meanwhile by a dense fog further thickened by smoke shell and bombs from Artillery, Aeroplanes and Mortars. The attack was so timed that the Left Bde of the 50th Division coming from a south-westerly direction should arrive at the railway embankment on the LE CATEAU - BASUEL Road simultaneously with the Right of the South African Bde. The attack of the South African Bde came as a complete surprise to the enemy, who was unaware that it had crossed the river. The enemy fought hard. The position was a very strong one and there were three belts of double apron fencing to be negotiated - undeterred, the South African Brigade carried out its task and secured its objective. The 6th R.D.F. of 198th Bde were detailed to mop up LE CATEAU by a concentric attack. This difficult work was most thoroughly accomplished with great dash. 198th Bde interposed one Battalion on the final objective between S.A. Bde and 50th Division on the Right.
18th-19th Oct.	On the night of 18th/19th Oct. the 199th Bde took over the Divisional front and pushed out certain posts in front of the RED Line on the 20th. Between 17th and 19th Oct. 4 Officers (including one Battalion Commander) and 265 O.Rs of 17th Reserve Division had been taken, also 2 .77 guns, 81 M.Gs., 5 lorries and 3 bicycles.
20th Oct.	On the night of the 20th/21st the 18th Division relieved 66th Division.

2. The following are some of the points to which attention must be paid next time :-

(i) Communications. The axial line of communication is undoubtedly the only satisfactory system, and when properly run is invaluable. The same method must be applied in advance of Brigades where the communication arrangements were poor. Battalion runners had to go excessive distances which could have been obviated by the provision of Advance Report Centres.

(ii) Reports. The standard varied considerably. Ignorance of the situation in many instances caused

/unnecessary....

2. (ii)(cont.)
unnecessary delay and in several cases casualties to our own troops. Commanders of units must ensure by using every means at their disposal that they are in touch with the situation on their own fronts. Officers patrols were not enough used in this respect.

(iii) In future, no barrage will be put down in answer to S.O.S. Signal by day or night, and a protective barrage after gaining final objective will seldom be employed, as both these cramp the style of the Infantry.
    F.O.Os will be attached to attacking battalions and will keep more in touch with the situation in the front line. They will regularly report direction of any hostile shelling for information of counter-battery work. Generally one Battery R.F.A. will be attached to each Brigade of Infantry, the Battery Commander usually remaining with the Brigade, and one Section being attached to each of the attacking Battalions. In this respect Training Leaflet No. 5 should be studied by all - it is being distributed down to Company Commanders.

(iv) <u>Evacuation of wounded.</u> Regimental Aid Posts will be pushed up closer to Battalions. This will allow of motor ambulances making full use of all passable roads and evacuating from as far forward as possible.

3. All ranks may justly be proud of the share they took in these operations, the great success of which was mainly due to :-

    (i)   The drive, marching and staying powers of the men.

    (ii)   The foresight and initiative displayed by junior officers and N.C.Os.

    (iii) The quickness with which all commanders adapted themselves to the constantly changing situation and the rapidity with which orders were issued and carried out

    (iv) The excellent co-operation of Artillery, Machine Guns, Tanks, Aeroplanes and Cavalry with the Infantry which largely contributed to the great pace with which the pursuit was pushed by the latter.

    (v)   The first rate performance of the R.E. in bridging the River SELLE, which alone rendered the trying operation of October 17th feasible
        The good work done by the 9th Glouc. R. (Pioneers) throughout the operations both in making a dry weather track and holding MONTAY.

    (vi) The untiring efforts of all the administrative services, resulting in the rapid evacuation of wounded, troops being fed, and ammunition supply secured.

    (vii) The excellent spirit which pervaded all ranks in all conditions. In itself always a deterrent to sickness, it resulted in the number of sick in the Division being extremely small, some units being almost free from any wastage from this cause.

D.H.Q.,
24th October 1918.

Major-General,
Commanding 66th Division.

WAR DIARY.

5th (Serv) Bn. Rl. Inniskilling Fus.

PERIOD.
1st to 30th November 1918

VOLUME No XL

CONFIDENTIAL

23.F

WAR DIARY or INTELLIGENCE SUMMARY.

Army Form C. 2118.

November (1.)

Place	Date	Hour	Summary of Events and Information	Remarks and references to Appendices
PREMONT	1.		Coys under Coy. Comdrs. for musketry & drill — afternoon bathing & Regt. Baths	
	2		Battalion moved to HONNECHY and billetted	
HONNECHY	3.		Battalion moved to LE CATEAU and billetted	
LE CATEAU	4		Marched to POMMEREUIL	
POMMEREUIL	5.		Left POMMEREUIL at 0745 and marched to join L.G.S.b. moved heavily during march — am 1945 Battn. arrived to LANDRECHIES & billetted	
LANDRECHIES	6		Arrived at NOVELLES at 1600. Road all the way very bad road	
NOVELLES	7		Marched from NOVELLES to DUNKIERRE arriving at 1945 Battalion marched to J.3.a.9.2. followed by "B" March Coy. to bn. Hors. J.m.c. 9.5 & 9.5.a.1.9 relief complete at 2250	

WAR DIARY
or
INTELLIGENCE SUMMARY.

(Erase heading not required.)

Army Form C. 2118.

Place	Date	Hour	Summary of Events and Information	Remarks and references to Appendices
J.3.c.9.2.	8.		Battalion attacked at 0730. "B" & "D" Coys in line "A" Coy reserve. B's H.Q. at Juction of J.3.c.9.2. & J.3.c.9.2. The advance continued rapidly until the Coys cleared the stream opposition from enemy M.G. fire was encountered particularly on the right. O/C 0840 centre Coy reports they were held up by M.Gs. O/C 0850. Right Coy reports they were held up. Enemy M.G. fire from the left front about J.6. a.6.4. but were still but enemy J.6.c.9.3. J.12. a.6.2. & J.12.a.6.4. On ops they afar of the reached the TAVASNES – ST AUBIN Rd. and were unable to advance owing to having the front from a line of 0930 L/P Coy on their right. Wood about D.10.6. to J.12. Reft. Coy reached objective (Canal AUBENES – MAUBEUGE) Road down to L/P. Coy. L/P. Coy up to a line of stopped put in a barrage to keep off an enemy attack up Centre Coy ar 1130 they began to advance up to that objective which the reached at 1200. The B & P. Coys	

was still held up but a/c stability lights needed the objective at 12.45. Found was gained with the 6/? Black B? in the 17th troops during the day to objective. At 14.00 6? [illegible] Bn. [illegible] to y Batt. was withdrawn to [illegible] of the [illegible] through
14.30. Batt. arrived back to [illegible] reserve in N.1.C. [illegible] Total casualties during operation 7 O.R. killed 29 O.R. wounded. Whilst held in reserve [illegible] slight ordnance the close vicinity of the country of the objective encountered — 1 N.C.O. 1 art 2 [?] men [?] 1 Anti. [?] 1 Transt. roller + 1 Officer + 1 O.R. were captured by the B.C. [?]
Batt. pushed up 09.00 to avoid [?] enemy [?] [illegible] then attack — 09.30 [illegible] Germans [?] [illegible] Batts. ordered back to V.B. aye.

WAR DIARY
or
INTELLIGENCE SUMMARY.
(Erase heading not required.)

Army Form C. 2118.

Place	Date	Hour	Summary of Events and Information	Remarks and references to Appendices
J.6.a.	10.		B⁺⁺ noted in enemy - at 1830 B⁺ connected to COPREAUX FARM by sent over line E. 28.d.5.6 K.U. 2nd. K.10. 2nd. - position by 2230	Appx 1
COPREAUX FARM.	11.	1000	received orange & stating ammunition & rations & take effect from 11.50. B⁺⁺ informed on firing a/c 11.10.	Appx 2
"	12	0900	Moved to SARS POTERIES & billeted	Appx 3
SARS POTERIES	13		Coys at disposal of Bay. Commrs. for cleaning up etc etc	Appx 4
"	14	4pm	Battalion marched to CLAIRFAYTS and billeted. O.Ps. handed in Guard of Honour to Corps Commdr (Gen Sir H. Rawlinson)	Appx 5
CLAIRFAYTS	15		Battalion inspected by G.O.C. commdy Brigade	Appx 6
"	16		Cleaning up etc : arriving - Working party of 120 O.R. to SOURE LE CHATEAU - arriving - D.A/R of 15 - 4 O.R. arrived	Appx 7

WAR DIARY or INTELLIGENCE SUMMARY

Army Form C. 2118.

Place	Date	Hour	Summary of Events and Information	Remarks and references to Appendices
CLAIRFAYTS	17.		Divine Service – Draft inspected by C.O. at 1630	J.E.
"	18.		Marched to FRANCE (Belgium)	J.E.
FRANCE	19.		Marched to PHILIPPEVILLE. Left FRANCE at 0815 reached PHILIPPEVILLE at 1400. Rdy onwd. Very heavy 1 O.R. fell out going away to find a road.	J.E.
PHILIPPEVILLE	20.		Battalion inspected in marching order by Commanding Officer	J.E.
"	21.		One Coy. working on road SILENRIEUX – PHILIPPEVILLE and remainder of Coys. at disposal of Coy. Comms. for instruction.	J.E.
"	22.		Battalion working on ROLEE – PHILIPPEVILLE road up to Sect. 16.	J.E.
	23.		Marched from PHILIPPEVILLE to MORVILLE. Battalion forming Advance Guard to 198 Inf. Bde.	J.E.

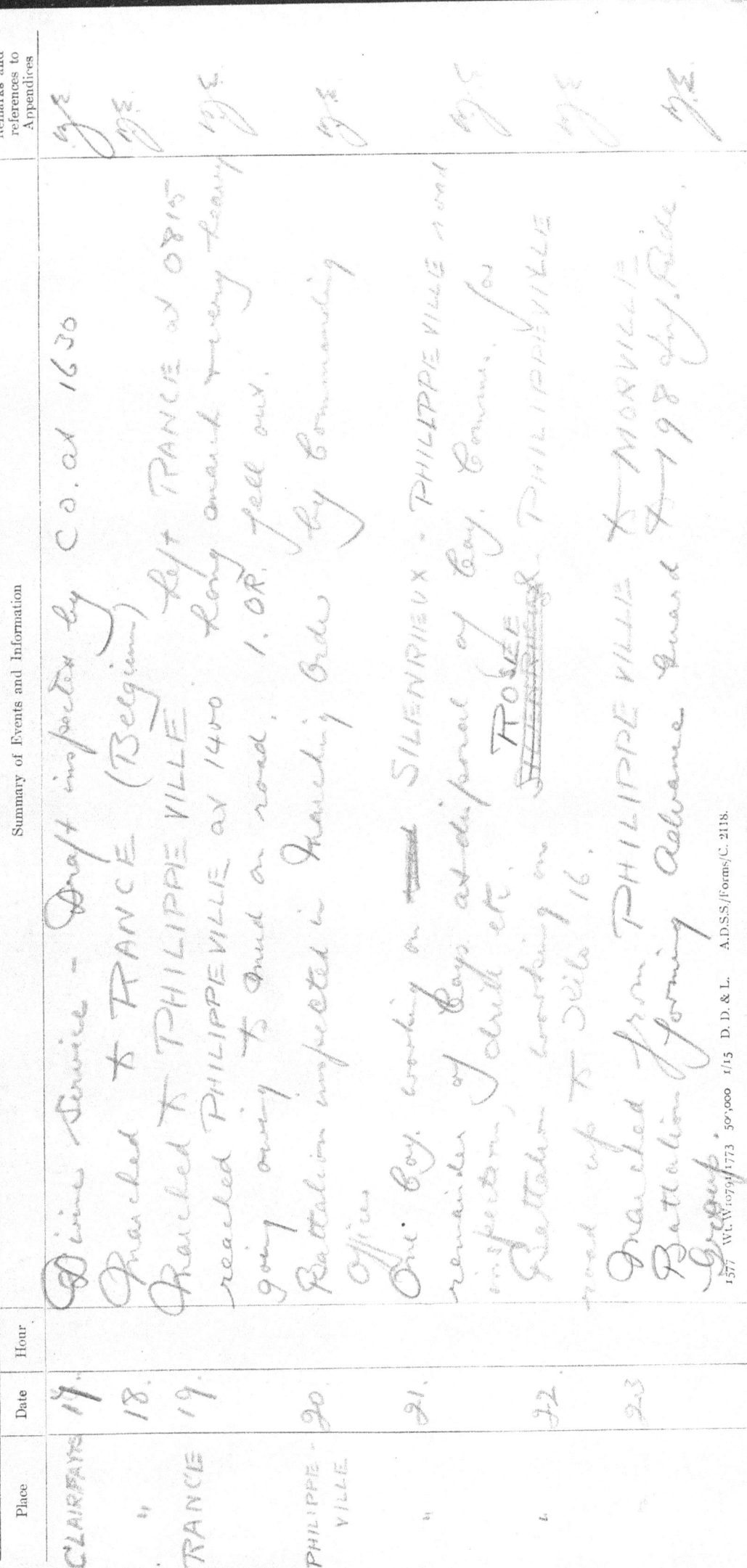

WAR DIARY
or
INTELLIGENCE SUMMARY.

Army Form C. 2118.

Place	Date	Hour	Summary of Events and Information	Remarks and references to Appendices
MORVILLE	24.	0830	Battalion paraded marched to HASTIERE-par-Dela on R. MEUSE	J.E.
HASTIERE par-Dela	25.		Coys at disposal of Coy. Commanders for cleaning up. Arms drill parade etc.	J.E.
"	26.		Company Drill Arms drill	J.E.
"	27.		Route march saluting drill	J.E.
"	28.		Companies at disposal of Coy. Comm. for ceremonial Coy drill	J.E.
"	29.		Short Route march Inspections	J.E.
"	30.		P.T. Arms drill saluting drill under Coy arrangement.	J.E.

J.S. Cowper Lt Col
Comdg. 5th (Ser.) Bn. Rl. Inniskilling Fus.

WAR DIARY

5th. (Ser.) Bn. Rl. Inniskilling Fus.

PERIOD

1st to 31st December 1916

VOLUME No XLI

CONFIDENTIAL

WAR DIARY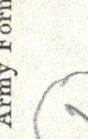

or

INTELLIGENCE SUMMARY.

(Erase heading not required.)

Army Form C. 2118.

December.

Place	Date	Hour	Summary of Events and Information	Remarks and references to Appendices
HASTIERE par-delà	1.		Divine services	JS.
"	2.		Companies at disposal of Offs Commanding Coys. for inspection, short route march etc.	JS.
"	3.		Coys. bathing at HASTIERE Station	JS.
"	4.		Arms drill, Coy drill inspection.	JS.
"	5.		Battalion cleaning harness, army aim repairs to roads.	JS.
"	6.		Church in village & afternoon route march. Battalion did a 7 mile route march.	JS.
"	7.		Coys. at disposal of OC. Coys. for drill etc	JS.
"	8.		Divine service — Coys. bathing at HASTIERE Station & armoury	JS.
"	9.		Coys. cleaning harness, arms, repairs to roads in village	JS.

Army Form C. 2118.

WAR DIARY
or
INTELLIGENCE SUMMARY.
(Erase heading not required.)

Place	Date	Hour	Summary of Events and Information	Remarks and references to Appendices
HESTIERE- par-dela	10.		Coys. at disposal of Coy. Commrs. for Drill, inspection etc. Active Service Army School in full swing. Attendance good.	
"	11.		Battalion route march. Half hour Coy. Drill on conclusion of march.	
"	12.		Coys. at disposal of Coy. Commrs. for Drill, inspection in afternoon. Medical inspection in afternoon.	
"	13		Battalion cleaning up any arrears upon return in Area.	
"	14		Route March	
"	15		Battalion marched to HOUYET and billetted	
HOUYET	16.		Battalion marched to ROCHEFORT. Very long march of 21 kilos. Rained intermittently, everything very wet. 1 O.R. (Pnly) fell out.	

Army Form C. 2118.

WAR DIARY
or
INTELLIGENCE SUMMARY.
(Erase heading not required.)

Place	Date	Hour	Summary of Events and Information	Remarks and references to Appendices
ROCHEFORT	17.		Coys. cleaning up & settling into billets	nil
"	18.		Fitting of equipment, Tactical Recce parade	nil
"	19.		Inspection of Lewis Gun equipment. Coys. cleaning up etc.	nil
"	20.		P.T. Arms Drill, cleaning up for G.O.C. inspection	nil
"	21.		Inspection of Battalion Rickets Jay G.O.C.	nil
"	22.		40 Gunners proceeded to U.K. for Demobilization. Divine Services	nil
"	23.		Short Route March	nil
"	24.		Coys. at disposal of OC Coys.	
"	25.		Christmas day.	nil
"	26.		Guard of Honour of 100 men furnished & were inspected by Rodier of Webs at ROCHEFORT	nil

Army Form C. 2118.

WAR DIARY
or
INTELLIGENCE SUMMARY.
(Erase heading not required.)

Instructions regarding War Diaries and Intelligence Summaries are contained in F.S. Regs., Part II. and the Staff Manual respectively. Title pages will be prepared in manuscript.

Place	Date	Hour	Summary of Events and Information	Remarks and references to Appendices
ROCHEFORT	27		Coy Arm Drill.	ME
"	28		Short Route March - Coy Drill	ME
"	29.		Divine Service	ME
"	30.		Coy Arms Drill	ME
"	31.		Short Route March - Coy Drill	ME

Fred B. Paterson Lieut Colonel
Comdg. 5th (Ser.) Bn. Rl. Inniskilling Fus.

War Diary
1st Royal Inniskilling Fusrs.
— Period —
1st to 31st January 1916
Volume XLII

Army Form C. 2118.

WAR DIARY
or
INTELLIGENCE SUMMARY.
(Erase heading not required.)

January

Place	Date	Hour	Summary of Events and Information	Remarks and references to Appendices
ROCHEFORT	1.		Coy Arms Drill	
"	2.		Route March. Company Drill.	
"	3.		Company Drill & Coy Drill.	
"	4.			
"	5.		Divine Service	
"	6.		Coy Drill - Arms Drill	
"	7.		Coy Drill & Arms Drill	
"	8.		Route March & musketry	
"	9.		Battalion proceeded by train to Marckh to witness a Rugby football match between the South African Brigade & Australian Division.	
"	10.		Battalion Paraded to practice presentation. Divine Inspection.	
"	11.		Coy Drill & Arms Drill.	

Army Form C. 2118.

WAR DIARY
or
INTELLIGENCE SUMMARY.

(Erase heading not required.)

Instructions regarding War Diaries and Intelligence Summaries are contained in F. S. Regs., Part II. and the Staff Manual respectively. Title pages will be prepared in manuscript.

Place	Date	Hour	Summary of Events and Information	Remarks and references to Appendices
ROCHEFORT	12		Divine Service.	8AM / 6PM
"	13.		Ceremonial Drill	
"	14.		Route March - Inspection of Transport by Divisional Commander	
"	15.		Ceremonial drill	EA2A
"	16.		Coy Drill	EA5B
"	17.		First day of Platoon Efficiency Competition - at TEMPLE. Battalion represented by no. 12 Platoon (C Coy.) Transport & entraining. Battalion not - needed.	
"	18.		Second test day of P.E. Competition, involving tactical schemes & Platoon training. No. 12 Platoon doing - gun jambed at first round. Coy + arm drill for remainder of Battalion.	
"	19.		Coy. & Ceremonial drill	
"	20.		Cres - country run. Each Coy. as strong as possible.	
"	21.		Coy. & Arms Drill.	
"	22.		Battalion paraded at Rendez-Vous in fast kit of drained transport	

Army Form C. 2118.

WAR DIARY
or
INTELLIGENCE SUMMARY.
(Erase heading not required.)

Instructions regarding War Diaries and Intelligence Summaries are contained in F. S. Regs., Part II. and the Staff Manual respectively. Title pages will be prepared in manuscript.

Place	Date	Hour	Summary of Events and Information	Remarks and references to Appendices
ROCHEFORT	23		Route - march. Village-quarters throughout him of much moveable property.	
"	24		Inspection by B.G.C. 198th Inf. Brigade of Battalion Billets. (1000 - 1200 hrs.)	
"	25		Salvage-operations continued. Practice by Brigade of Formation for move to new S.E.?	
"	26		WX of KENNEL Relief 5 billets 1500 hrs. Lt. Col. A.W.S. Paterson D.S.O. returned from leave & resumed command of Battalion. Church Parade.	
"	27		Company Games &c.	
"	28.		Rifles Hds — H.Q. training afternoon. Games evening continued. Trained teams for C.F.D. by S.	
"	29		Trained teams A.B.C.D. by S. in morning.	
"	30		Route march, in honor of Practice presentation of minor things.	
"	31		Brigade ceremonial on presentation of minor things. Snow again fell.	

1/2/19.

A.W.S. Paterson Lt Col
Comdg. 5" R. Inniskilling Fus.

CONFIDENTIAL

WAR DIARY

OF

5th (Ser.) Bn. Rl. Inniskilling Fus

FROM FEBRY 1 – 28 / 1919.

VOL 43.

Army Form C. 2118.

WAR DIARY
or
INTELLIGENCE SUMMARY.
(Erase heading not required.)

February

Place	Date	Hour	Summary of Events and Information	Remarks and references to Appendices
ROCHEFORT	Feb 1.		A Coy entrenching farm of Boche trenches. Remainder cleaning up & from south of ROCHEFORT.	
	2.		Divine Service parade.	
	3.		Wire clearing by A, B & C Coys.	
	4.		Entrenching of farm by O.C. D Coy — return to billets finished.	
	5.		Snow clearing by A & C Coys. on ROCHEFORT - CINEY road. Ridges between D Coy & Bn. H.Qrs. of position. Fall of snow 3" in night.	
	6.		Snow clearing by B & D Coys. from kilo 45-47 on ROCHEFORT-CINEY road. 1 platoon to entrain wagons on to big sleds.	
	7.		No C Coy & 1 platoon of D Coy in entraining teams of sleds inwards.	
	8.		Coys. 3-8 Platoons undertook Bosche Train. Bn.Hq. at b/o H.E. having F.A. available.	

WAR DIARY
INTELLIGENCE SUMMARY

Army Form C. 2118.

Place	Date	Hour	Summary of Events and Information	Remarks and references to Appendices
ROCHFORT	February 9		Church Parade.	
	10		No. I Coy. & all available men of No. II Coy. entrenching train. Bathe entrained.	
	11		Capt. G.M. visited M.G. amm[unitio]n section of 1/5th Composite. No. 1-6 Platoons continued entrenching of train.	
	12		All available men of No. I Coy. entrenching train. No. 2 Coy. will mentioned.	
	13		No. 2 Coy. & all available men of No. I Coy. shortly work in entrenching train. Battn. Coy. visited No. I & No. II Coy. M.G.C. at HAMERSIR in Divisional Football Competition.	
	14		No. I Coy. will available of No. II Coy. entrenching train.	
	15		No. 1-6 Platoons entrenching train	
	16		Church Parade. Battalion beaten by Div. M.T. Coy. at CINEY in final of Divisional Football Competition, ground under water in many places.	
	17		Nos. 3-8 Platoons entrenching train.	

Army Form C. 2118.

WAR DIARY
or
INTELLIGENCE SUMMARY.
(Erase heading not required.)

Instructions regarding War Diaries and Intelligence Summaries are contained in F. S. Regs., Part II. and the Staff Manual respectively. Title pages will be prepared in manuscript.

Place	Date	Hour	Summary of Events and Information	Remarks and references to Appendices
Rochefort	18		Nos 1 - 6 Platoon unloading Train Nos 7 - 8 Nothing	M.E.
"	19.	0215	296 O.R. paraded & marched to JEMELLE STN. en route to U.K. for Demobilization. 6 Officers proceeded in Conducting Duty with party.	M.E.
"	20		Camp billets evacuated by party demobilized.	M.E.
"	21		Party proceeded to BUISSONVILLE to load abandoned enemy shells on to Lorries return to ROCHEFORT Salvage Dump.	M.E.
"	22		Inspection of Billets	M.E.
"	23		Divine Service	M.E.
"	24		Remaining men re-organized into two Coys. No. 1 Renamable. On Coy Armies of Occupation. No. 2. Bath Cadre men for release	M.E.
"	26		Coys. as deployed of 66. Coy. completing re-organization	M.E.

WAR DIARY
or
INTELLIGENCE SUMMARY.

Army Form C. 2118.

(4)

Place	Date	Hour	Summary of Events and Information	Remarks and references to Appendices
Rochefort	26	0215	32 O.R. proceded to JEMELLE en route to U.K. Demobilisation	mjs
"	27		Coys. at disposal of O.C. Coys. No. 1. Coy. bathing	mjs
"	28		No. 2. Coy. bathing. Coys at disposal of O.C. Coys.	mjs

A.W.S. Patterson Lt Col
Cmdg 5th (Ser.) Bn. Rl. Inniskilling Fus.

CONFIDENTIAL.

WAR DIARY

OF

5TH Royal Inniskillings Fus.

From MARCH 1ST. TO MARCH 31ST.

VOLUME No 44.

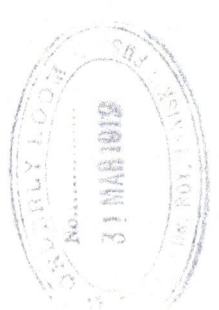

Army Form C. 2118.

WAR DIARY
or
INTELLIGENCE SUMMARY.

(Erase heading not required.)

March (1)

Instructions regarding War Diaries and Intelligence Summaries are contained in F. S. Regs., Part II. and the Staff Manual respectively. Title pages will be prepared in manuscript.

Place	Date	Hour	Summary of Events and Information	Remarks and references to Appendices
ROCHEFORT	1.		Coys. at dispersal of Regt. Common.	7.
"	2.		Divine Service. 5 officers 100 O.R. paraded at 17.00 marched to JEMELLE to entrain en route to join 1/5 Batt. R. Inniskilling Fus.	7.
"	3.		Cleaning. Leers evacuated by draft.	7.
"	4.		Arrived by lorry from Rochefort dront. Left 11.00 arrived 13.08	7.
SOVET	5.		Cleaning up. Voting in letter	7.
"	6.		Six O.R. proceeded to U.K. for demobilisation	7.
"	7.		Coys. at Regt. Common. dispersal	7.
"	8.		All officers NCOs attended lecture by Major Gen. Montgomery K.C.B. a Return of Waterloo at CINEY	7.

Army Form C. 2118.

WAR DIARY
or
INTELLIGENCE SUMMARY.
(Erase heading not required.)

Instructions regarding War Diaries and Intelligence Summaries are contained in F. S. Regs., Part II. and the Staff Manual respectively. Title pages will be prepared in manuscript.

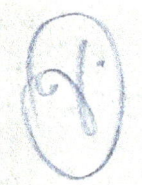

Place	Date	Hour	Summary of Events and Information	Remarks and references to Appendices
SOYET.	9.		Divine Service	
"	10.		All men employed under Q.M. cleaning out Retr. wash stands etc. to return to Ordnance	
"	11.		As for 10th	
"	12.		Coy fatking and disposal of Coy. Common Inspection of billets.	
"	13.		Bath at Chipanne by Rate.	
"	14.		All men employed with Q.M. cleaning wagons etc.	
"	15.		M.O.R. re engaged proceeded to U.K. for Furlough	
"	16.		"St Patrick's Day". All men Coln - Horse bath	
"	17.			

WAR DIARY or INTELLIGENCE SUMMARY.

Army Form C. 2118.

Place	Date	Hour	Summary of Events and Information	Remarks and references to Appendices
SOYET	18.		Brattn of HAM-sur-LESSE report - a very enjoyable day	J.S.
"	19.		Lorries parades to convey men to the Due Race CINEY.	J.S.
"	20.		Coys. at disposal of O.C. Coys for inspection etc. Inspection of billets & medical inspection	J.S.
"	21.		Officer commanding & OC proceeded to WATERLOO by lorry to be taken over battlefield.	J.S.
"	22.		Inspection etc. Divine Service	J.S.
"	23.		All are employed cleaning arms etc to be	J.S.
"	24.		Rested in quarters	J.S.

Army Form C. 2118.

WAR DIARY
or
INTELLIGENCE SUMMARY.
(Erase heading not required.)

Place	Date	Hour	Summary of Events and Information	Remarks and references to Appendices
SOYET	25.		Inspection & completing of draft proceeding to 1/8th Bn R. Inniskillings Fus.	
"	26.		22 O.Rs. proceeded to join 1/8th Batt. R. Inniskillings Fus. Batt. strength now 14 Officers 50 O.Rs.	
"	27.		Cleaning billet evacuated by men who left to join 1/8 o Bn R. Inniskilling Fus.	
"	28.		Cadre Bathing at Divisional CINEMA proceeded by lorry	
"	29.		Inspection etc	
"	30.		Divine Service + 9 O.R's proceeded to U.K. for re-engagement	
"	31.		Case. Bn. strength (present with unit) 18 Officers 46 O.Rs.	

Calway Capt
Commdg 4th (S) Bn Royl. Innis. Fusiliers

CONFIDENTIAL

WAR DIARY for APRIL 1919

5TH ROYAL INNISKILLING FUSILIERS

VOL XLV

Nov 16

28.I

Army Form C. 2118.

WAR DIARY
or
INTELLIGENCE SUMMARY.
(Erase heading not required.)

April (1.)

Instructions regarding War Diaries and Intelligence Summaries are contained in F. S. Regs., Part II. and the Staff Manual respectively. Title pages will be prepared in manuscript.

Place	Date	Hour	Summary of Events and Information	Remarks and references to Appendices
SOVET	1.		Cadre bathing at Div. HQrs CINEY	y.s.
"	2.		Inspection of billets, all available men cleaning roads etc	y.s.
"	3.		Inspection parade	y.s.
"	4.		Inspection of billets	y.s.
"	5.		All men employed under Qr Mr. cleaning roads by Bn. HQ Store	y.s.
"	6.		Cadre moved to CINEY v/LETTRE. Lorries reported at 1000 hrs. Move completed by 1200.	y.s.
CINEY	7		Settling into new billets	y.s.
"	8		Inspection of billets	y.s.
"	9.		Rifle & kit inspection	y.s.

Army Form C. 2118.

WAR DIARY
or
INTELLIGENCE SUMMARY.
(Erase heading not required.)

Place	Date	Hour	Summary of Events and Information	Remarks and references to Appendices
CINEY	10.		All NCO's & men of Bath parade & marched to Divisional Bath.	
"	11.		Interior Fatigues on.	
"	12.		Billet and Billetry inspection	
"	13.		Divine Service	
"	14.		Maj.L. 99 Offrs HH ORs	
"	15.		Rifle & Kit inspection	
"	16.		At Offrs & ORs proceeded to UK for demobilization	
"	17.		re-enforcement base. Strength 20 Officers 41 ORs	
"	18.		Good Friday - Divine Service.	

Army Form C. 2118.

WAR DIARY
or
INTELLIGENCE SUMMARY.
(Erase heading not required.)

(3)

Place	Date	Hour	Summary of Events and Information	Remarks and references to Appendices
CINEY	19.		Cadre Inspection of Bde. Iron Transport - afternoon	
"	20.		Bathing Parades	
"	21.		Inspection of billets	
"	22.		Rifle + Equipment inspection	
"	23.		5 Officers + ORs to F.G War Conference return of Staff Capt to Base	
"	24.		Reg'tl Officer 15. ORs 35.	
"	25.		Billet Alarm inspection	
"	26.		Cadre Bathing	
"	27.		Divine Service	
"	28.		Inspection of equipment, arms tables	

Army Form C. 2118.

WAR DIARY
or
INTELLIGENCE SUMMARY.
(Erase heading not required.)

(4)

Place	Date	Hour	Summary of Events and Information	Remarks and references to Appendices
CINEY	29		Cadre catching	
"	30		All available men today were equipped to join training battalions & rest to U.K. for tomorrow. Strength of Cadre 4 Officers 37 O.R.	

D.D. Galway Capt
Commg 5 Northumberland Fus.

CONFIDENTIAL

War Diary

5th Ryl Inniskilling Fusiliers

May 1 – 9. 1919

Army Form C. 2118.

5th Royal Inniskilling Dragoons

WAR DIARY
or
INTELLIGENCE SUMMARY.
(Erase heading not required.)

May, 1919.

Place	Date May	Hour	Summary of Events and Information	Remarks and references to Appendices
CINEY	1		Entraining of limbers & wagons began at 0900 hrs and the entire got through at 1700 hrs. The entire of 6½ kmscuits drawn & A. & B. Sqs. of M.G.S. on same train. V. wet.	
ANTWERP	2.		Arrived at ANTWERP at 0600, and after unloading vehicles and storing them in a hanger on aerodrome marched to No. 2 Evacuation Camp on outside of town 800x— Camp almost submerged. Remainder of day spent in settling into huts — subsequent missed huts.	
	3		A Spring-bog at C.Inf. Inspection & cadre & horse at 0900 hrs. Marched Inspection at 1130 hrs. Rest of day spent in	
ANTWERP	4.		ANTWERP Inspection of cadre and tillet at 0900 hrs. Passes issued all O.R.S from 1400 hrs — midnight, permanent travel inspection at 0900 hrs. Perfect weather.	
	5.		Cadre piquet-work.	
	6			
	7		after morning inspection at 0900 hrs — day spent by majority in	
	8		ANTWERP V. Sup.	

Army Form C. 2118.

5th Royal Inniskilling Fus.

WAR DIARY
or
INTELLIGENCE SUMMARY.
(Erase heading not required.)

May 1919.

Instructions regarding War Diaries and Intelligence Summaries are contained in F. S. Regs., Part II. and the Staff Manual respectively. Title pages will be prepared in manuscript.

Place	Date	Hour	Summary of Events and Information	Remarks and references to Appendices
ANTWERP	9		May 8 morn. Loading of vehicles	
		1330 hr.	Proceeded by tender onboard at 1545. Loading began at 1130 hr. & finished at 1545. hrs. on S.S. PRETORIAN.	

D J Eaton Capt
Comdg D Coy 5th Royal Inniskilling Fusiliers

Army Form C. 2118.

WAR DIARY
or
INTELLIGENCE SUMMARY.

(Erase heading not required.)

Place	Date	Hour	Summary of Events and Information	Remarks and references to Appendices

Instructions regarding War Diaries and Intelligence Summaries are contained in F. S. Regs., Part II. and the Staff Manual respectively. Title pages will be prepared in manuscript.

www.ingramcontent.com/pod-product-compliance
Lightning Source LLC
Chambersburg PA
CBHW081439160426
43193CB00013B/2323